MENTAL HEALTH AND CONFLICTS

A Handbook for Empowerment

Published by DRI Press, an imprint of the
Dispute Resolution Institute at Mitchell Hamline School of Law.

Dispute Resolution Institute
Mitchell Hamline School of Law
875 Summit Avel St Paul MN 55105
Tel. (651)695-7676
© DRI Press. All rights reserved.
Printed in the United States of America
Library of Congress Control Number: 2025915411
ISBN-13: 978-1-7349562-9-0

Mitchell Hamline School of Law in Saint Paul, Minnesota has been educating lawyers for more than 100 years and remains committed to innovation in responding to the changing legal market. Mitchell Hamline offers a rich curriculum in advocacy and problem solving. The law school's Dispute Resolution Institute, consistently ranked in the top dispute resolution programs by *U.S. News & World Report*, is committed to advancing the theory and practice of conflict resolution, nationally and internationally, through scholarship and applied practice projects. DRI offers more than 30 dispute resolution courses each year along with two certificate options. Established in 2009, DRI Press is the scholarship dissemination arm of the Dispute Resolution Institute which brings significant conflict resolution work to a broad audience. For more information on other DRI Press publications, visit https://mitchellhamline. edu/dispute-resolution-institute/dri-press/

Cover design by Karin Preus/Acorn Design.

MENTAL HEALTH AND CONFLICTS

A Handbook for Empowerment

DAN BERSTEIN

DRI PRESS

Saint Paul, Minnesota

DEDICATION

This book is dedicated to everyone who makes an effort to empower others, and especially those people who helped me make my own choices when I was vulnerable due to my mental illness.

Our Commitment to Making This Book Affordable and Accessible

When *Mental Health and Conflicts: A Handbook for Empowerment* was first published by the American Bar Association in 2022, they priced it at $99.95 - a rate that was not affordable for many who wanted it.

DRI Press and Dan Berstein are united in their commitment for mental health inclusion and empowerment. We decided to make this book available as widely as possible without cost becoming a barrier to anyone who may be able to use its lessons and tools to help them during their conflicts and mental health situations.

The 2026 DRI Press edition is available for free electronically at www.mhsafe.org/mhc. We also worked to create the lowest feasible price we could for its physical publication via Amazon KDP, taking into account their restrictions and DRI Press's costs to prepare and publish the book. Lastly, we included additional new, free bonus resources with this new 2026 edition of the book

Table of Contents

PREFACE FOR THE 2026 DRI PRESS EDITION

I am grateful to DRI Press for collaborating to develop and publish this new edition of *Mental Health and Conflicts: A Handbook for Empowerment.*

In 2022, when the American Bar Association (ABA) published the original book, it represented a culmination of my life's work including stories from my lived experience of five hospitalizations for bipolar disorder, insights from my academic pursuits studying Mental Health at the Johns Hopkins School of Public Health, and practical resources developed during a decade of professional experience working at the intersection of dispute resolution and mental illness.

The final manuscript succinctly summarized all of the lessons I had learned relating to the ABC's of Mental Health and Conflicts:

- **A. Accessibility**

  Providing trauma-informed, universally-designed options for people to get support for their mental health needs without being pressured to disclose their private personal information.

- **B. Boundaries**

  Responding to challenging behaviors in consistent, impartial, and effective ways without stigmatizing mental illnesses or profiling people who may have them.

- **C. Communication**

  Recognizing the plethora of personal choices people have about their mental health and communicating about them in empowering ways.

I was proud the book blended practical tools, academic knowledge, and personal stories so others would hopefully be able to quickly learn all of the important takeaways from my life.

❖

The next chapter of my life began the week I turned in the book manuscript to the ABA. I saw some inappropriate content posted about mental illness on a community listserv and I decided to reply explaining why it was wrong. The person accused me of "playing the mental illness card" and they petitioned to have me barred from responding, invoking dangerousness stereotypes about mental illness, including writing "I feel stalked."

It broke my heart to realize that no matter how hard I worked or credentialed myself, it would still always be so easy for people to disparage me with stigmatizing comments related to my mental illness. I decided I had to do more than teach the ABC's of good mental health communication. I had to keep speaking up to help people stop disseminating mistakes in their guidance.

That week, I registered the website to launch the Mental Health Safe Project (MH Safe)—and I began contacting people and organizations so they could stop the three inappropriate I's:

- **Invasions**

  Conducting exams, assessments, or inquiries that inappropriately or illegally seek private disability information.

- **Impediments**

  Providing disparate treatment to people who seem to have mental impairments, profiling them to deny them service, provide less communication, or otherwise diminish their opportunities.

- **Inaccessibility**

  Creating stigma, burdens, and backlash in response to requests for disability accommodations.

This work has been rewarding and impactful. Recently, the MASIC-S and Michigan State Courts removed screening questions about mental illness, the Association for Conflict Resolution removed safety guidance suggesting people with mental illnesses were violent and spent years developing new bias-resistant materials, and the authors of the famous Harvard book *Difficult Conversations: How to Discuss What Matters Most* worked with Penguin to revise their already-released new edition to remove material suggesting people with mental illnesses are difficult. Those are just a few of many examples of important, far-reaching changes that would never have happened without this book and my ensuing advocacy. You can see more examples at www.mhsafe.org/mhc.

As meaningful as this advocacy work has been, the past four years have also been incredibly difficult for me interpersonally as well, and have taken a toll on my mental health. The ABA was once a great supporter of my work—showcasing numerous awareness programs and articles about preventing discrimination, publishing my book, and allowing a member of their General Counsels' Office to work with me to make changes to remove harmful content from an ABA podcast, an event description, and books (content that had inappropriately singled out people with some disorders for stigmatizing reactions and disparate treatment). And yet the interpersonal struggles and bipolar symptoms I faced amidst my advocacy work also led me to become alienated from some important staff at the ABA. I wound up terminated from the organization and barred from all of their programming—and the book's copyright was returned to me as well.

❖

Mental Health and Conflicts: A Handbook for Empowerment begins with a message that we all have mental health needs and it ends with a focus on how we all have bad days. My experiences these past four years have been filled with difficult moments that caused distress for me and many others, including the folks who arranged for my termination from the ABA.

Conflicts affect all of our mental health, and—while some people are managing disabilities like mine and others are dealing with less severe day-to-day difficulties—we all fall short of our best during our difficult moments.

We can learn to do better if we continue developing best practices for accessibility, boundaries, and communication (ABC's) and if we prevent the three inappropriate I's. This book can help anyone do exactly that.

❖

This new version, from DRI Press, is more accessible than ever. I am thankful that we have been able to work together to re-publish it, and I hope it helps you.

I am also working on a sequel book that will provide a Toolkit for Distress. While this book provides information and resources to help anyone do the right thing when it comes to mental health and conflicts, I realized it does not acknowledge how hard it is to do the right thing. People are often, understandably, avoidant or reluctant to change or just plain overwhelmed. The sequel book will provide research and tools to help people anticipate and navigate their distress in collaborative ways so, hopefully, no one will have to suffer as much in situations like the challenges I faced with the ABA and other organizations.

You can help by sharing your questions, stories, or requests for skills via a quick anonymous survey that you can also access at www.mhsafe.org/mhc.

INTRODUCTION: WE ALL HAVE MENTAL HEALTH NEEDS

We all experience conflicts every day—with our families, our friends, our coworkers and even within ourselves. Whether the conflicts you are experiencing last moments or years, and whether you are able to handle them on your own or you need outside help, all conflicts are about more than the specific options being debated. Every person in a conflict brings their own individual needs to the table.

This handbook presents frameworks for anticipating and addressing mental health needs in conflicts. Its lessons can help laypeople as well as professional conflict resolvers, people living with mental health problems as well as people with no knowledge of mental health, and those dealing with conflicts that are specifically focused on mental health as well as those facing any other kind of conflict.

We start with the simple premise that mental health needs are relatable. All of us know what it is like to have a bad day. We have each been sad, worried, or overwhelmed. We understand that conflicts can be hard and that they can often bring out the worst in us.

As easy as it is to realize we all have mental health needs, we also must accept that mental health is complicated. Close to half of us will experience a diagnosable mental health problem at some point in our lives, but no two people ever experience a mental health problem the exact same way. Everyone forms their own personal beliefs about their mental instability, and they make their own choices about how to address it.

That is why this book begins by defining mental health and mental illness through diverse lenses instead of a single, one-size-fits-all definition. We will learn to respect a variety of viewpoints and emerge with an ability to be sensitive to each individual's unique experiences.

Next, we will explore how mental health concerns arise during conflicts. Sometimes the topic is out in the open from the very beginning because the conflict pertains to a mental health condition. For example, conflicts may arise about whether someone feels they are being discriminated against because of their mental health diagnosis or because of debates about whether someone should pursue a certain kind of care. This book will prepare you for these kinds of cases.

Other times the conflict may not relate at all to a mental health issue, but a party will choose to disclose it. They may be generally open, like I am with my bipolar disorder, or they may be asking for the help they are entitled to under the Americans with Disabilities Act. Either way, this book will prepare you to handle these disclosures.

Unfortunately, mental health labels often get tossed out as accusations during conflicts. Sometimes this is frivolous name-calling, while at other times it is meant sincerely as a way to try to help. There are also times it can happen as a part of a deliberate campaign to undermine a person's credibility. In this book we will cover each of these scenarios.

The last and most common way mental health concerns arise in conflicts is through our own suspicions. When things feel difficult and behaviors escalate, we may start to wonder if there is something more to the story. This book gives us the tools to manage our own biases so that we can still be empowering despite our concerns.

In order to effectively handle these disclosures, accusations, and suspicions, it is important that we first dispel some dangerous myths about mental health needs. We will take on the assumptions, paternalism, and stigma that undermine communication related to mental health. We will also discuss why people often scapegoat mental health conditions instead of addressing the broader challenges that weaken our conflict resolution processes.

Many people believe the myth that it is our responsibility to figure out if someone has a mental health diagnosis, or use our knowledge of their actual diagnosis, so that we can help them. We will talk about the actual role of a conflict resolver and the appropriate ways to work with mental health labels. We will shift our thinking away from making our own guesses about who might need special help and we will move toward providing support opportunities to all parties in a conflict—recognizing that anyone may have a mental health need at any time and that it is not appropriate for us to try to figure it out.

Perhaps the most stigmatizing myth about mental health problems is that people with these problems exhibit challenging behaviors such as an inability to communicate or a propensity for violence. In this book, we will discuss how these kinds of biases hurt the entire conflict resolution process, and we will cover how to manage challenging behaviors impartially, independent of any possible backstory about a person's mental health.

By the end of this book, you will have the tools you need to be empowering regardless of someone's mental health circumstances.

You will learn to talk about mental health in validating ways without falling into the common pitfalls of making assumptions about someone else's preferences or experiences.

You will have access to universal design frameworks that you can use to make your process accessible and supportive to people with many different mental health needs—all without requiring anyone to disclose them to you, and all without you having to make guesses about who needs what.

Finally, the challenging behavior tools described in this book will help prepare you for all kinds of emergencies, disruptions, and disconnects without ever linking those behaviors to someone's mental health situation. This will help you treat everyone fairly without singling anyone out.

Mental health can be confusing. This handbook teaches the three techniques you need to navigate that confusion without inadvertently becoming insensitive, offensive, or discriminatory. By learning how to talk about mental health in empowering ways, how to be accessible to people with diverse needs, and how to address challenging behaviors based on behavioral criteria, you will be ready to support anyone's mental health needs in conflicts.

People often think I need special help because I have been hospitalized with bipolar disorder, and they often believe that the lessons I teach are only valid for people with mental illnesses as serious as mine. It is not common for people to disclose their conditions as I have, so we have to assume that anyone could be like me. Anyone you speak to, at any time, could be privately dealing with a serious mental illness, or they might not yet realize they are going to eventually experience one. At a minimum, we all need to learn these lessons so that we can treat all people as if they might privately have a condition like mine.

But it is also important that we move beyond that minimum. We can start to recognize that every person on the planet falls somewhere on a single, universal spectrum of mental health. I hope you will find that this handbook on mental health needs in conflicts is not just applicable to the many people who have serious mental illnesses like mine. We all have mental health needs, and this book can help you support **anyone** in conflict.

An Orientation to This Book

A Note about My Personal Stories

In addition to the research and case studies cited in this book, I am also including some of my personal stories of living with bipolar disorder. I share these stories first and foremost because research shows that contact education is superior to other approaches to change peoples' behavior regarding mental illness stigma.[1] In other words, the best way to develop an open mind to the spectrum of mental health experiences is to get to know someone who has a mental disorder.

I am also sharing my personal stories as a reminder to you that I myself am a biased source of information about mental health. One key message from this book is that we all have our own unique, evolving perspectives about mental health. Mine is just one of them, and it is admittedly not neutral because I am merely a human being, and all people make mistakes.

Like you, I have unconscious biases that I do not even realize, and my decisions are shaped by my experiences, sensitivities, and values. That is why I believe it is vital for all of us to aspire toward impartial, universal processes that constrain our behavior and limit the impact of our unknown prejudices. This book focuses entirely on developing those neutral procedures so that we can have empowering, validating interactions that are open-minded toward all kinds of mental health experiences and points of view.

I am open about my point of view in hopes that it will help you adapt these techniques to fit your own perspective. I am presenting you with options and choices instead of one-size-fits-all answers. My hope is that the work I have done as a mediator and mental health expert living with bipolar disorder will resonate with you, as will this book's message of developing impartial processes.

How This Book Is Structured

Because this is a handbook, I want to make it easy for you to turn to it as a reference resource. For this reason, each chapter is built using the following elements:

Chapters

The main content of each chapter is designed to function as a lesson introducing a core concept.

---

[1] National Academies of Sciences, Engineering, and Medicine. (2016). *Ending discrimination against people with mental and substance use disorders: The evidence for stigma change.* National Academies Press; Stuart, H. (2016). Reducing the stigma of mental illness. *Global Mental Health, 3.* https://www.ncbi.nlm.nih.gov/pmc/articles/PMC5314742/.

Takeaways

Throughout each chapter, key insights will be framed as Takeaways. These tips are meant to be helpful touchstones for you to incorporate into your practice. They are also collected as a reference in the Takeaways section at the end of the book.

Personal Stories

When I share a story based on my lived experience with bipolar disorder, it will typically be in sections labeled as my personal story.

Case Studies

Three types of case studies are included in this book, all of which are drawn from my work or my research. The case studies include examples from family conflicts, workplace situations, and conflict resolution settings.

Tools

My company, MH Mediate, has worked to adapt the concepts included throughout this book into succinct, user-friendly tools that can help people during their regular practice. I intersperse these tipsheets, checklists, templates, and talking points as resources throughout the book.

Scenarios

At the end of each chapter, I share practice scenarios or exercises for you to imagine your response applying the lessons of this book. In order to give you a chance to reflect on your own, the scenarios are presented without guidance from me as to the proper answers. This gives you an opportunity to apply the lessons from the chapter and use its principles to reason out how you might respond to these situations.

The Role of the Reader

One major theme of this book is that, before we can prepare for any kind of conversation or conflict about mental health, we must be mindful of our personal role in the matter.

This book is designed to teach concepts and tools relevant to all kinds of mental health needs and situations. While we focus on three major categories of examples—family situations, workplace situations, and professional conflict resolution situations—the lessons we cover are universal, and they are broadly applicable.

Because this book is meant to serve people across a variety of facets of life, I do not presume to know exactly what your role is going to be. Accordingly, it is especially important for you to personally reflect on your role as you read this book. I include some tools and prompts to help you do so because knowing your role is the key to discovering the best path forward through any conflict.

If you are a family member, is it your role to provide some kind of support, share interpersonal boundaries for cohabitation, or share concerns? If you are a coworker, is your role to ensure productivity and a good workplace climate? If you are a professional conflict resolver, are you supposed to protect each person's voice, choice, and sense of fairness? Perhaps your role is different from these examples. Whatever your role is, this book will shine a light on how to speak in empowering ways without overstepping one's boundaries.

That is an important consideration because too often, when people look for mental health resources they inadvertently begin to overstep. In most cases, it is inappropriate to assess someone else's mental health condition, render a clinical diagnosis, or suggest treatment solutions. Remembering our role can help us focus on what is appropriate to discuss without inadvertently violating someone's boundaries.

In Part II of this handbook, we debunk a variety of myths about mental illness that have led to the assumptions, stigma, paternalism, and scapegoating that unfortunately infiltrate so many of our interactions about these complicated topics. This book will serve as a journey to help you understand how you can best communicate within your role without any overstepping. You will come to see that the communication techniques we cover are profoundly simple at their core. The hard part is stepping back from the mindset that it is your job to assess another person's mental health or fix their problems.

Following the processes outlined in this book can be easy, and talking about mental health can be relatively anxiety-free, as long as you remember your role.

Appreciating Discrimination

Discrimination occurs when one person receives different treatment than another based on the perception that the person belongs to a different category of people.

Just as people can experience discrimination based on their race, gender, age, religion, or sexual orientation, so they may also experience discrimination based on having a disability, including a mental health condition. Discrimination toward people with disabilities is generally known as ableism, while discrimination focused specifically on mental health disabilities is called sanism.[2]

This book teaches people ways to empower those with mental health conditions rather than provide them disparate treatment. Many of the practices are designed to prevent unintentional discrimination that may occur due to unconscious biases.[3] To overcome these biases, we will explore approaches rooted in procedural fairness or procedural justice.[4] The goal is to provide a process that is fair regardless of the stigma and bias that may otherwise lead to disparate treatment of someone with a mental health condition.

I mention different examples of discrimination throughout this book. Unless I say so specifically, I am not providing an evaluation as to whether a specific act of discrimination will create legal liability.

By way of introduction, I will now provide a general overview of the dynamics of mental illness discrimination, the laws related to it, and how these laws are enforced. Researchers have found that this discrimination can be structural and that it can include both intentional and unintentional acts.[5] Note that I am not an attorney, and this is not legal advice meant to help you understand your legal liability. Rather, this section provides a broader conceptual understanding of what might constitute discrimina-

---

[2] Perlin, M. L. (1992). On sanism. *SMUL Review, 46,* 373.

[3] Izumi, C. (2017). Implicit bias and prejudice in mediation. *SMUL Review, 70,* 681.

[4] Rawls, J. (2020). *A theory of justice.* Harvard University Press.

[5] Corrigan, P. W., Markowitz, F. E., & Watson, A. C. (2004). Structural levels of mental illness stigma and discrimination. *Schizophrenia Bulletin, 30*(3), 481–491.

tion and how it could potentially lead to liability. The goal is to provide a wider context about why these concepts matter.

At its most basic level, people may harbor or express stigmatizing attitudes in the form of mental illness microaggressions that often are not illegal. These microaggressions include everyday snubs, slights, and insults connoting denigrating messages that may suggest the target is inferior, scary, shameful, second-rate, or disingenuous about their difficulties.[6] These offensive communications will not necessarily be coupled with overt acts of discrimination. Therefore, they may not ever lead to any legal liability unless, perhaps, they become so severe or pervasive as to give rise to emotional distress or a hostile work environment.[7] A record of these negative attitudes could also become supporting evidence to bolster claims of discriminatory acts that violate the law.

What does amount to illegal discrimination? The answer depends on the law at hand, as well as how it is being enforced. Many state and federal laws protect people with disabilities from disparate treatment. The Department of Justice's *Guide to Disability Rights Laws* includes references to the Americans with Disabilities Act (ADA), the Telecommunications Act, the Fair Housing Act, the Air Carrier Access Act, the Voting Accessibility for the Elderly and Handicapped Act, the National Voter Registration Act, the Civil Rights of Institutionalized Persons Act, the Individuals with Disabilities Education Act, the Rehabilitation Act, and the Architectural Barriers Act, just to name a few pieces of legislation.[8] Thus, there are protections at work, in public places, for voting, housing, and across most other settings and services.

Perhaps the easiest way to understand the massive scope of possible discrimination affecting people with disabilities is to refer back to President George H. W. Bush's remarks when he signed the ADA into law in 1990.[9] He made it clear that this legislation was meant to have a pervasive impact rippling through our entire society. He explained that the ADA was designed to stop the rampant discrimination and segregation affecting people with disabilities by protecting them from unequal treatment and removing access barriers preventing them from achieving equal participation across all areas of life.

These admirable aspirations have never been completely fulfilled because actual legal liability for disability discrimination is dependent on a wide range of factors. The ADA's enforcement has varied over time, with changes that happen across different presidential administrations, implementation regulations, Supreme Court decisions, congressional amendments, and advocacy efforts to bring claims.[10] Some research indicates that people with psychiatric disabilities do not fare well in ADA claims, and it even suggests that there may be some discrimination in the due process that people with mental ill-

---

[6] Gonzales, L., Davidoff, K. C., Nadal, K. L., & Yanos, P. T. (2015). Microaggressions experienced by persons with mental illnesses: An exploratory study. *Psychiatric Rehabilitation Journal, 38*(3), 234.

[7] von Schrader, S. (2018). Research brief: ADA employment discrimination charges citing harrassment. Northeast ADA Center at Cornell ILR. Retrieved from https://ecommons.cornell.edu/handle/1813/90125.

[8] U.S. Department of Justice Civil Rights Division (2020). A Guide to Disability Rights Laws. Accessed from https://www.ada.gov/cguide.htm.

[9] Bush, George H. W.(1990). Remarks of President George H. W. Bush at the Signing of the Americans with Disabilities Act. Retrieved from https://www.ada.gov/ghw_bush_ada_remarks.html.

[10] Dorfman, D., & Burke, T. (2020, December 7). Thirty years later, still fighting over the ADA. The Regulatory Review. https://www.theregreview.org/2020/12/07/dorfman-burke-thirty-years-fighting-over-ada.

ness receive for their discrimination claims.[11] People also do not always realize they can make claims. Researchers reviewing misconduct claims in mediation suggest that parties often do not have enough awareness to hold mediators accountable for misconduct because they do not understand that misconduct even occurred. Their solution was a Party Bill of Rights—a document that educates all parties in a mediation about their rights so that people will realize they can make a claim when they notice bad behavior.[12]

The practical reality of discrimination liability is complicated and constantly evolving. This book is not designed to educate anyone about quantifying legal risks, making discrimination claims, or defending against them. Rather, it is acknowledging that stigma, unconscious bias, and microaggressions all have the potential to manifest as discrimination and increase the risk of legal accountability. To the extent that preventing liability is a motivator, the tools in this book may help you reduce discrimination because they are designed to help you achieve procedural fairness in the way you discuss mental health, address challenging behaviors, and implement accessibility practices.

But remember: the law is the bare minimum standard of justice. We can all hold ourselves to a higher ethical standard that goes further than merely avoiding legal accountability. There is no ceiling on how much we might aspire to empower everyone we encounter, and there is no such thing as treating anyone with too much dignity. We can continually use the resources in this book to allow people with mental health differences to achieve full equity and inclusion.

This Book Is a Prism

It is important to approach this book with the understanding that a primary goal is to open your mind to diverse views about mental health. You are still entitled to hold all of your views, just as I still have mine, but when we take on the role of resolving a conflict, we must be ready to listen to others and mitigate our own biases.

This book is designed to help you do that. Much of the content is meant to hit the reader as a prism—shattering any singular point of view someone has about mental health and mental illness, and expanding their perspective to reveal an infinite spectrum of valid mental health experiences. In order to do this, you may notice that some themes are repeated, some examples overlap, and some material is shared through multiple modalities. This is an example of the accessibility principles we will review in chapter 8, functioning as a way to ensure that people of different learning styles all have some way to connect to the content.

We must humble ourselves every day if we are to let go of our biases and preconceptions. I started this book by humbling myself to you and acknowledging that I am still limited by my own point of view. The best any of us can do is acknowledge this never-ending spectrum of perspectives, and try our hardest to stay open-minded and fair.

---

[11] Swanson, J., Burris, S., Moss, K., & Ullman, M. (2006). Justice disparities: Does the ADA enforcement system treat people with psychiatric disabilities fairly? *Maryland Law Review, 66,* 94.

[12] Bultena, C., Ramser, C., & Tilker, K. (2019). Mediation madness V: Misfit mediators. *Southern Journal of Business and Ethics, 11,* 53–75.

PART I

UNDERSTANDING MENTAL HEALTH NEEDS

As you will discover from this first part of the book, there is no single universal definition of mental health. We will explore a variety of different frameworks, definitions, and explanations. As you learn to appreciate some of the terminology debates that divide different mental health communities, you will also see that underneath these disagreements there lie common threads that unite all of us on the same, broad spectrum of feelings, thoughts, and behaviors.

As we embark on the path of understanding how to work with mental health needs in conflicts, it is important to remember that all of us have mental health needs. We may not all call them that—and none of us will have the exact same story as anyone else. That can make things confusing, especially if we search for "right answers" about someone else's potential mental health problems.

This section of the book steers you away from those kinds of definitive answers. Instead, we focus on exploring a wide variety of choices, perspectives, and definitions of mental health, as well as some common situations when the topic may arise in conflicts. The continuing goal is to keep an open mind about mental health and defer to each individual's personal perspective. We are setting the stage for listening to others, respecting their points of view, and appreciating the choices they make in their lives as well as during conflicts.

CHAPTER 1

WHAT ARE MENTAL HEALTH AND MENTAL ILLNESS?

The world of mental health is a confusing one. Part of what makes mental health issues so complicated is that different communities have different ideas in mind when they define mental health and mental illness.

In fact, although mental health is a very broad term that seems to have wide acceptance, many people continue to disagree with the idea that our emotional well-being is tied to our brain. Therefore, they disagree with the term entirely. Similarly, even though the phrase "mental illness" has such a robust history that it has been codified into some major organizations' names such as the National Alliance on Mental Illness, for many people this term has been seen as stigmatizing.

So what are we to do, then, if we are trying our best to be sensitive and aware of mental health needs in conflicts? We must be careful and open-minded with our terminologies.

This first chapter of this book begins with an introduction to some of the more common terms and definitions related to mental health and mental illness. Rather than leave you with a single, narrow lens, this chapter seeks to open your eyes to a spectrum of meaning; that way you will be ready to listen to the various perspectives people have. You will also be more prepared to navigate the confusion and conflicts that can emerge from those differences. To that end, we will explore a wide variety of experiences and choices available to people as they embark on their own personal journeys of understanding their mental health needs and managing their mental health problems.

A. MENTAL HEALTH

The World Health Organization (WHO) defines mental health as "a state of well-being in which an individual realizes his or her own abilities, can cope with the normal stresses of life, can work productively and is able to make a contribution to his or her community."[13] Put simply, mental health is universal. It is our social, emotional, and psychological well-being. It is about having healthy thoughts, feelings, and behaviors.

While this definition may seem comprehensive, there are people who have a different view. Galderisi et al. (2015) explains how the WHO definition made progress by focusing on the positive aspects of mental well-being as opposed to merely defining mental health as the absence of mental health prob-

---

[13] World Health Organization (2018). Mental health: Strengthening our response. Retrieved from https://www.who.int/news-room/fact-sheets/detail/mental-health-strengthening-our-response.

lems.[14] However, they believed the WHO definition was too constrained by specific cultural norms putting pressure on positive experiences.

Their inclusive definition is as follows:

Mental health is a dynamic state of internal equilibrium which enables individuals to use their abilities in harmony with universal values of society. Basic cognitive and social skills; ability to recognize, express and modulate one's own emotions, as well as empathize with others; flexibility and ability to cope with adverse life events and function in social roles; and harmonious relationship between body and mind represent important components of mental health which contribute, to varying degrees, to the state of internal equilibrium.

If you are thinking that this definition is a mouthful, I agree. Don't worry—you don't have to learn it. This is just one of a seemingly endless cascade of potential definitions that vary depending on the person, profession, or community with which you are dealing. Remember, we are talking about how to look at mental health and *conflicts*, so we have to start by recognizing that there are conflicting views about how to define mental health in the first place.

Many organizations and practitioners believe in focusing on aspects of wellness, with eight dimensions serving as a commonly used framework: emotional, spiritual, intellectual, physical, environmental, financial, occupational, and social.[15] These dimensions are seen as interdependent factors that impact well-being. Again, there is no conclusive one-size-fits-all model of understanding mental health. What is important is not to arrive at such an answer, but rather to be prepared to listen to the perspectives of whoever is in the conflict instead of judging their perspective by your own values. For the purposes of this book, we will treat any need we encounter as potentially falling on the spectrum of mental health.

Anyone who seems sad, worried, or overwhelmed by a conflict may have mental health needs. If you are a mediator and you see someone getting red in the face while the other person is talking, that may be a mental health need. If you are at work and someone is absent a few days in a row, that could be due to a mental health need. Friction among family members at Thanksgiving? It sounds like there may be mental health needs there too.

Of course, we are just keeping an open mind to the endless possibilities of people experiencing mental health needs. It is not our place to assume there actually is one unless that is something the parties themselves indicate. Later in this book, we will learn to take accessible approaches to deal with anyone's needs while keeping an open mind. You will learn to hear each individual's perspective of mental health instead of inserting your own, so you can respectfully listen to their point of view even if they disagree with the framework of mental health entirely.

Mental health needs can be expressed in many different ways. Just remember: they have to do with how people find their own balance when managing their thoughts, feelings, and behaviors. In other words, mental health touches all facets of our lives, and mental health needs can be virtually any needs.

---

[14] Galderisi, S., Heinz, A., Kastrup, M., Beezhold, J., & Sartorius, N. (2015). Toward a new definition of mental health. *World Psychiatry, 14*(2), 231.

[15] Swarbrick, M. (2006). A Wellness Approach. Psychiatric Rehabilitation Journal, 29(4), 311–314; Stoewen, D. L. (2017). Dimensions of wellness: Change your habits, change your life. *The Canadian Veterinary Journal, 58*(8), 861.

TAKEAWAY

All needs can be seen as mental health needs, and everyone might have their own unique definition of mental health. Generally, mental health relates to all dimensions of well-being, with an emphasis on thoughts, feelings, and behaviors.

i. Dimensions of Wellness

It is important to keep in mind the scope of mental health needs, and how they permeate every aspect of our lives. That is why we will take a moment to identify the eight core dimensions of wellness, each of which are interrelated with our mental health and linked to our mental health needs. Remember, this is just one of many possible frameworks and conceptions of mental health. We are using it because it is a helpful way to appreciate a variety of types of mental health needs.

Emotional

Emotional wellness includes your sense of your own feelings as well as the ability to appreciate those of others. It also involves being able to manage emotions constructively and maintain a sense of emotional balance and positivity about life. Emotional well-being is inextricably tied to our mental health because it is linked to how we manage feelings and how we develop healthy behaviors.

Spiritual

Spiritual wellness is focused on developing your personal values, understanding your purposes, and feeling a sense of meaning. It also includes participating in any activities that are supportive of your values and beliefs. It does not necessarily have to include any religious beliefs. Rather, in this sense, spirituality is a sense of connectedness, depth, and meaning. Viktor Frankl wrote a book called *Man's Search for Meaning*, explaining his theory that the sense of purpose is the foundation of one's mental health. He quoted Nietzsche's belief that "he who has a why can endure any how."[16]

Intellectual

Intellectual wellness is linked to anything we do to nurture our minds. It includes aspects such as being curious, feeling challenged, growing our perspectives, learning, increasing knowledge, and sharing these gifts with other people. Intellectual wellness is related to mental health because our intellectual performance is linked to how we are feeling.

---

[16] Frankl, V. E. (1985). *Man's search for meaning*. Simon and Schuster.

Physical

Physical wellness focuses on the well-being of your body. It includes decisions related to diet, exercise, sleep, and health care services. All of these activities are vitally connected to mental health because any change in physical well-being can affect moods, thoughts, and behaviors.

Environmental

Environmental wellness pertains to all sorts of environments outside yourself. This includes your social atmosphere, the natural environment, and the built environment. It can also include a commitment to supporting the health of the planet and being part of sustainability efforts.

Financial

Financial wellness involves developing healthy plans for earning, saving, spending, and investing, as well as realistic goal-setting and the development of a sense of financial security and preparedness.

Occupational

Occupational wellness is all about fostering a sense of self-esteem, productivity, and purpose from your work. It can include a professional job as well as other kinds of work, such as volunteering, and the focus is on doing these things in a way that provides a sense of satisfaction as well as a feeling of using your gifts and talents productively.

Social

Social wellness is related to all kinds of relationships in your life—family, friends, and intimate relations as well as a general sense of plugging into your community. When someone is socially well, they care about others, and they also welcome others caring about them.

ii. Visualizing Life Choices Worksheet (Tool)

This worksheet can be used as part of a discussion to understand a person's life choices related to different aspects of their mental health. You may use this tool as a way to reflect on someone's choices prior to a mediation or an important conversation, as a prompt to ask them to share more about each dimension, or as a way to reflect on their perspective afterward.

For each dimension of wellness, highlight the relevant choices that each individual has:

Emotional

Spiritual

Intellectual

Physical

Environmental

Financial

Occupational

Social

iii. Family Mental Health

Many of the examples in this book will explore conflicts that affect families. Family mental health takes on a few special considerations of its own. For starters, it is important to recognize that each person within a family has their own personal mental health, but the family itself, whether it is united or fragmented, has its own sense of mental health.[17] You can apply the same eight dimensions of wellness to an entire family at once, instead of just using it for each of the individual members.

This book explores ways to be respectful to the different mental health choices made by individuals and their different contexts. Likewise, each family can be seen through the lens of the broader cultures that comprise it and the norms of the family itself. Each family has its own history of choices and experiences and beliefs that become a way to understand its mental health. Families may have experienced their own shared traumas in the past which also relate to their mental health.

iv. Workplace Mental Health

Workplace examples are also a focus of this book, so it is important to take a moment to introduce some considerations about workplace mental health.

Workplaces may have different office cultures regarding how proactive they are in offering mental health support for their employees, as well as in providing resources and benefits designed to increase overall well-being. Similarly, there is a spectrum of work/life balance and stress levels that varies from organization to organization. In these ways, it is possible to take the pulse of the overall mental health or climate of a specific workplace culture across the eight dimensions framework, just as we can do with a family.

Workplace mental health interventions may include efforts to promote positive mental health, prevent harm, and manage any mental illness that occurs.[18] A workplace can promote mental health by reducing stressors at work or promoting positive feelings.

v. Personal Story: Talking Mental Health

People often confuse the idea of mental health with mental illness (the subject of the next section). Early on in my career, I developed and presented mental health assembly programs for middle and high school students, with a goal of encouraging them to pay more attention to their mental health. I began each presentation with an exercise where I asked people to raise their hands if they checked how they looked in the mirror this morning before leaving the house, or whether they paid any attention to their aesthetics. Usually, virtually all of the hands would spring up. Then I asked if they did anything to take care of their mental health. Did they engage in any kind of check-in to see how they were feeling emotionally? Typically, few or no people would raise their hand, except for the occasional class that was from a more religious community. Those students often mentioned prayer as a way they had to check in with themselves about how they were doing.

---

[17] Broderick, C. B. (1993). *Understanding family process: Basics of family systems theory.* SAGE.

[18] LaMontagne, A. D., Martin, A., Page, K. M., Reavley, N. J., Noblet, A. J., Milner, A. J., & Smith, P. M. (2014). Workplace mental health: Developing an integrated intervention approach. *BMC Psychiatry, 14*(1), 1–11.

When I visited schools, I would share the story of how I was diagnosed with bipolar disorder when I was 19, after I experienced a severe manic episode. That episode filled me with a dysfunctional burst of energy that kept me up for four days straight and culminated in my earnestly believing I was going to travel back in time to fix it so my parents would not get divorced.

That condition is a mental illness called a mood disorder, and the episode was a cluster of different symptoms of that illness. As we will learn in the next section, that means it was a problem with my thoughts, feelings, and behaviors. Because I experienced this problem, I was hospitalized and forced to take a semester off from college. I then began a long, difficult journey to access treatment and pursue my recovery.

While I visited the schools to help reduce the stigma associated with mental illness, my primary focus was on sharing the idea that we all can do things to take care of our mental health. I would share how my recovery allowed me to feel better than ever. I explained that I never realized that growing up had been hard for me, with a lot of bottled-up pain that I had carried with me every day. I never knew to even think about changing my feelings, but treatment for my mental health condition opened my eyes to the possibility that we can improve.

I would say, "It is sad that it took having a mental illness for me to finally pay attention to my mental health." The treatment efforts that I pursued for my bipolar disorder helped me achieve a peace of mind that I never had growing up. That's because I never knew I could improve across the eight wellness dimensions. I did not understand that I had mental health at all. My constant hope was that the students could realize the potential value of paying attention to theirs.

B. MENTAL ILLNESS

As hard as it is to agree on language to define mental health, there is even less of a consensus about mental health problems. Generally speaking, a mental health problem is a problem thinking, feeling, or relating to others. The problem disrupts someone's life and lasts a long time. The exact definition varies based on clinical diagnosis, and it can be complicated by people having different viewpoints and conceptions about what qualifies as a mental health problem or how to label it. Even among experts, there are wide chasms of disagreement that stretch to every possible extreme, with some believing devoutly in the latest diagnoses and others lobbying for change.

Many different perspectives in mental health have emerged in part because there is uncertainty regarding the science underpinning mental disorders. The science is very young, and, for almost all conditions, the causal pathways are too poorly understood to definitively declare an understanding of what's happening. That means there is skepticism as to whether these labels really map onto discrete conditions at all, and treatments are typically determined through some form of trial and error rather than through doctors having derived a clear set of answers about why these treatments work on some people and not on others. Moreover, because symptoms are evaluated using self-reports and interpretations of behavior rather than through blood tests and brain scans, that inherently subjective process means that both people living with mental health problems and their clinicians are left with subjective ideas of what it means to feel better and how well a treatment might actually be working.

Recently, controversy has arisen over the validity of the *Diagnostic and Statistical Manual of Mental Disorders* (DSM-5).[19] This manual presents a taxonomy of mental disorders that was designed to be reliable rather than valid (meaning that most psychiatrists will agree that people meet the criteria for a specific syndromal disorder, but no one knows if that disorder truly exists).[20] Challenges to the disorders' validity have led to the National Institute of Mental Health's call for a new framework for classifying mental health problems based on dimensions instead of syndromes and spectrums instead of categorical labels.[21] It is not important for you to understand that debate. Rather, the point is to realize that there is much conflict even among medical experts in the world of mental health. Their ideas of mental health conditions are debated and in flux.

Beyond this tumult within the medical perspectives, there are other ongoing debates about mental disorders. Many mental health consumers depart from mainstream medicine's best practices, citing valid concerns such as side effects and high rates of treatment resistance (for example, studies have shown that 30–60% of schizophrenia cases and 12–20% of depression cases are treatment resistant).[22,23] In light of these consumer attitude shifts, researchers have begun moving from a model of adherence to one of self-determination.[24] Later in this chapter we will explore more of these choices in depth.

People may also have different beliefs about mental health problems due to their varying lived experiences. Perspectives differ across a plethora of dimensions, including an individual's role in the system and their views about the nature of the problem, rights, and appropriate treatments.

When we are approaching the subject of mental health, we are talking about people's feelings, thoughts, and behaviors. There is perhaps nothing more subjective or open to interpretation. This presents an immense challenge to someone in search of clear, objective facts and "right answers." Yet this ambiguity presents a great opportunity to someone who cares about understanding, addressing, and resolving conflicts. The absence of definitive wrong answers means we can truly do our best to listen to each person's perspective, treat it as valid, and integrate it into the larger story as we work through disagreements.

---

[19] American Psychiatric Association. (2013). *Diagnostic and statistical manual of mental disorders* (5th ed.). APA.

[20] Cuthbert, B. N., & Insel, T. R. (2013). Toward the future of psychiatric diagnosis: The seven pillars of RDoC. *BMC Medicine, 11*(1), 126.

[21] Insel, T., Cuthbert, B., Garvey, M., Heinssen, R., Pine, D. S., Quinn, K., & Wang, P. (2010). Research domain criteria (RDoC): Toward a new classification framework for research on mental disorders. *American Journal of Psychiatry, 167*(7), 748–751.

[22] Solanki, R. K., Singh, P., & Munshi, D. (2009). Current perspectives in the treatment of resistant schizophrenia. *Indian Journal of Psychiatry, 51*(4), 254.

[23] Mrazek, D. A., Hornberger, J. C., Altar, C. A., & Degtiar, I. (2014). A review of the clinical, economic, and societal burden of treatment-resistant depression: 1996–2013. *Psychiatric Services, 65*(8), 977–987.

[24] Corrigan, P. W., Angell, B., Davidson, L., Marcus, S. C., Salzer, M. S., Kottsieper, P., & Stanhope, V. (2012). From adherence to self-determination: Evolution of a treatment paradigm for people with serious mental illnesses. *Psychiatric Services, 63*(2), 169–173.

TAKEAWAY

Stay open to different ways that people may conceptualize their mental health problems, if they even see them as problems at all. Defer to their views and be sure to validate them.

C. DSM-5 DISORDERS

Because the DSM-5 is the source of diagnostic labels used by health insurance companies and clinicians alike, these are the conventional mental disorder labels that you are most likely to encounter if you pursue mental health treatment or if someone identifies with a psychiatric disability or whatever they are calling a mental health problem. The DSM-5 contains over a hundred diagnoses complete with criteria lists to determine who qualifies for what.

Between the variables in each diagnosis and the potential for multiple concurrent diagnoses, it can get complicated. For the purposes of this book, I will just share a list of the broad categories of conditions included in the DSM-5:

- Neurodevelopmental disorders
- Schizophrenia spectrum and other psychotic disorders
- Bipolar and related disorders
- Depressive disorders
- Anxiety disorders
- Obsessive-compulsive and related disorders
- Trauma- and stressor-related disorders
- Dissociative disorders
- Somatic symptom and related disorders
- Feeding and eating disorders
- Elimination disorders
- Sleep–wake disorders
- Sexual dysfunctions
- Gender dysphoria
- Disruptive, impulse-control, and conduct disorders
- Substance-related and addictive disorders
- Neurocognitive disorders
- Personality disorders
- Paraphilic disorders

This list is just an overview to give you a sense of what mental health disorders can encompass. It is not presented here as a recommended classification scheme. Even mental health clinicians are often resistant to ascribing much validity to these labels, choosing to give their clients a diagnosis so that they can reimburse their care through insurance but also letting those clients know they are skeptical about relying on an imperfect labeling system. Some have even raised ethical concerns about whether it is okay for mental health professionals to use a diagnostic framework while they lack confidence in its scientific validity.[25]

While these clinicians are struggling to make peace with what they perceive to be a flawed system, many people living with mental health problems will share their diagnoses with pride. I am one of them: I include it in my professional bio and announce it to the world in many different ways on a regular basis. However, just because I identify with this label does not necessarily mean I agree with every tenet of the medical model of mental illness.

TAKEAWAY

Mental health problems can be confusing and complicated. The DSM-5 is an imperfect labeling system used differently by different people. Avoid assumptions when you hear someone share their diagnosis, and instead listen to their choices and preferences.

D. MENTAL HEALTH CHOICES

This book focuses on empowering everyone living with mental health needs. To do that, we must start by appreciating and respecting all of their choices. This section first explores when people may be unable to make their own choices to distinguish that severe circumstance from other times. Then we dive into the kinds of choices people make regarding their mental health so that we can have a foundation for respecting these decisions.

i. When Is It Appropriate to Override Someone's Choices?

One of the most dangerous things about mental health conditions is that they can, in fact, be disabling. Most of us are not mental health experts, but we are able to get the general sense that someone who is suffering symptoms from a mental illness may be making some choices they may later regret.

The question is: When are we entitled to voice our judgments about someone else's decisions? We each have different ideas of where those lines are. Is it okay, for instance, to express skepticism about someone's religious decisions, their political affiliations, the person they are dating, their chosen career, their eating choices, and so on? How is that line different for mental health choices? Is it different because a person experiencing mental instability may need help and not recognize it? Entire books have-

---

[25] Raskin, J. D., & Gayle, M. C. (2016). DSM-5: Do psychologists really want an alternative? *Journal of Humanistic Psychology, 56*(5), 439–456.

been written about this topic, with clinicians even coining the term anosognosia to describe when they believe someone does not have insight into the idea that they have a condition.[26]

In this book, we are always careful not to dismiss someone's point of view. Therefore, you will not find me labeling someone with anosognosia. Yet we still must be mindful that people are worried that folks are too sick to know better, and we must factor that concern into our thinking as we develop a framework for talking about mental health needs. We need to understand how to feel comfortable about the appropriate boundaries when looking at someone's capacity to make decisions, as well as the biases involved in that process. We look at that concern more deeply in chapter 5 when we explore the myth of people needing special help due to their mental health conditions.

For now, we need to keep a few considerations in mind about respecting someone's autonomy when they have a mental illness.

1. Unless a person meets the legal criteria to be involuntarily committed or under guardianship, they have the same rights to make their own decisions as anyone else.

2. People living with mental health conditions are legally protected from disparate treatment under the ADA.[27] That means that disregarding someone's decisions based on their mental health condition could be illegal.

3. If you are trying to help a person out of concern for their mental health, it is important to have supportive, empowering communication with them so that they do not end up alienated from you. Maintaining an empowerment mindset and showing them respect can help them decide they can eventually benefit from the support you have to offer, on their terms. That is the philosophy advised by a popular expert and clinician Xavier Amador, the creator of the LEAP method (Listen—Empathize—Agree—Partner) which guides folks in connecting with people who do not want help.[28]

TAKEAWAY

Regardless of whether you are worried about a person and whether you are worried about your legal liability, it is always important to show respect for someone's personal choices about their mental health.

[26] Prigatano, G. P. (Ed.). (2010). *The study of anosognosia*. Oxford University Press.

[27] Americans with Disabilities Act of 1990, Pub. L. No. 101-336, 104 Stat. 328 (1990).

[28] Amador, X., & Johanson, A. L. (2000). *I am not sick, I don't need help! Helping the seriously mentally ill accept treatment*. Vida Press.

ii. What Choices Can People Make about Their Mental Health?

When we talk about mental health and mental illness, the subject can seem straightforward. But the reality is that people can make many, many choices about their mental health. This section provides a few examples so you can be better prepared to be validating and respectful of any choices someone has made.

Beliefs as to the Nature of Mental Health Problems

Many people are familiar with the question of nature versus nurture in influencing a person's development. The issue of how much someone's biology versus their life experience impacts their mental health has similarly been the subject of debate. Most experts believe mental health problems are caused by some combination of an underlying vulnerability and external, environmental stressors.[29] Yet that dynamic can be interpreted in many ways, and there are still many people who believe that mental health problems are due to just biology or just environment or neither. In a world with so many different possible stories about why mental health needs exist in the first place, each individual—be they a layperson or a mental health clinician—ends up making choices about what they believe a mental health problem to be and how they believe it comes about.

Preferences for Labels, Diagnoses, and Other Language

It is important to ask what someone means when they use language to describe mental health rather than make assumptions about it. You will find there are many different kinds of mental health terms, which are covered later in this chapter. The important thing to remember is that people have choices about what language, terminology, and labels they use to describe a mental health problem. This applies to mental health clinicians too; they have choices they can make about how to assess and diagnose their clients, with many clinicians disagreeing with the DSM-5 and choosing an alternative way to appreciate and describe someone's mental health problems.

Types of Treatment to Pursue

Many different options are available for someone seeking support for their mental health needs. First, they can decide whether they want to seek out a mental health professional to find this support or whether they prefer to seek some other kind of counseling, such as faith-based counseling or life-coaching, or to look for other outlets for help with their mental health needs. Of course, they can also choose not to do anything at all.

If someone were to decide they wanted to consider medication for their mental health, they would have many choices of where to get such a prescription. They could visit a psychopharmacologist, psychiatrist, psychiatric nurse practitioner, primary care physician, and—in some places—a psychologist. Most of those professionals could also provide some kind of talk therapy, as could social workers or mental health counselors and some other types of treatment professionals. Because mental health can

---

[29] Hankin, B. L., & Abela, J. R. (Eds.). (2005). *Development of psychopathology: A vulnerability-stress perspective.* SAGE.

be so subjective, people are typically advised to look for a clinician with whom they feel some rapport. Thus, across all of these different possible types of professionals, within each niche people have a choice of which specific professional they feel is a good fit.

All of these various professions offer many different approaches for treatment. With medication, for example, someone could choose monotherapy (a single drug) or polypharmacy (a cocktail of multiple prescriptions), or none at all. They could also change their diet, sleep, and exercise patterns. There are many different kinds of talk therapies they could choose to pursue including psychodynamic therapy, cognitive-behavioral therapy, dialectical behavior therapy, and many others. All of these treatments can be delivered at different intensity levels: higher doses or lower doses of medication, higher frequency or lower frequency of therapy visits. People can make decisions about all of these variables, as well as what they want to talk about with their therapists and what they would rather keep to themselves.

Mental health treatment is not just limited to medical experts. There are many complementary and alternative medicine approaches for mental health.[30] While some professionals and others might scoff at these approaches, they do provide value for many people. Moreover, eventually scientists study them, and they often become part of mainstream treatment approaches. For instance, mindfulness meditation, which was originally seen as something that was not a serious treatment, ultimately became the cornerstone of much modern therapy thanks to studies that proved its therapeutic benefits for many people.[31]

The options available for someone to support their mental health are virtually endless. It is important to see these treatment options as choices people select rather than as definitive right answers.

Who They Want to Tell and What They Want to Tell Them

Anyone living with a mental health problem has Health Insurance Portability and Accountability Act (HIPAA) rights that protect their privacy. Thus, no one has an obligation to tell anyone else about their mental health experiences, and clinicians are legally prohibited from doing so unless that person chooses to waive this privacy right.[32] Beyond mental health problems, no one has a duty to share any mental health needs or feelings in a conflict or at any other time. We all always have a choice as to who to tell. That's important: as a conflict resolver, we must always remember that we have no expectation to ever be told anything about someone's mental health situation unless they choose to tell us.

If someone chooses to share any information, we must respect that they have a right to omit as much or as little as they would like from their story. They also could choose to tell white lies in order to protect themselves from facing mental health stigma (we will explore stigma in chapter 3). In addition, people can choose to tell someone things and then change their minds later. They are in the driver's seat regarding how they tell their story at all times.

---

[30] Mamtani, R., & Cimino, A. (2002). A primer of complementary and alternative medicine and its relevance in the treatment of mental health problems. *Psychiatric Quarterly, 73*(4), 367–381.

[31] Kuyken, W., Watkins, E., Holden, E., White, K., Taylor, R. S., Byford, S., & Dalgleish, T. (2010). How does mindfulness-based cognitive therapy work? *Behaviour Research and Therapy, 48*(11), 1105–1112.

[32] Letzring, T. D., & Snow, M. S. (2011). Mental health practitioners and HIPAA. *International Journal of Play Therapy, 20*(3), 153.

What Kind of Support to Seek

Workplaces, families, and conflict resolvers can choose to offer varying levels of support to people experiencing mental health needs. Whatever they offer, it is each individual's right to decide how much or how little support they will seek from their loved ones or workplace or any other people in their lives.

Some people may decide they want to live their life being treated the same as anybody else, and so they will seek no support and keep their needs private. Others may decide they want as much support as possible, so they are not limited or suffering in private. They may ask for a lot of help from family or make requests for disability accommodations at work. Legally, the ADA gives them special rights to ask for that extra support to enable their equal participation in the workplace or other areas of society. But just because they have these rights, that does not mean they have to exercise them—and just because they have families who want to give them support, that does not mean they have to rely on that support either.

These are difficult, complicated personal decisions. Someone might vacillate from feeling like they want to act like they need no support for years, only to later realize they do not want to carry so many burdens and change their philosophy. We must always respect everyone's choices regarding support and be open to supporting them if they change their minds.

What Kind of Lifestyle Someone Wants to Live

As we discussed earlier, every aspect of the eight dimensions of wellness affects someone's mental health. That means every lifestyle choice is connected to a person's mental health needs, and it is important for us to respect that people have every right to choose a lifestyle they prefer. That can include who they socialize with, what kinds of risk-taking behaviors they pursue, what type of and amount of work they do, where they live, and many other decisions.

Often when mental health needs are involved, people can become paternalistic and judgmental regarding someone's life decisions, given their vulnerability. To be effective and impartial conflict resolvers, it is important for us to keep an open mind when listening to anyone's lifestyle decisions. We must also be supportive that these items are always a person's personal choice rather than presume we know what might be "right" or "healthy" for them to do.

TAKEAWAY

People have lots of decisions they can make about understanding, labeling, and treating mental health problems as well as choices about communication, support, and their overall lifestyle. Our role as conflict resolvers is to respect that these are their choices to make rather than assess if they are healthy. People can choose to get advice about what may help them from treatment professionals, assuming they choose to pursue that treatment. However, it is not our place to form judgments or give advice as part of a conflict resolution process. Nor is it our place to let our judgments of their decisions bias how we treat them.

iii. Personal Story: A Tale of Two Doctors

Although it is often tempting to believe there are definitive "right answers" in mental health, the reality is there are many different choices. Many people end up not realizing all of their options. Thanks to my parents' divorce, I saw some of the choices right away.

When I was 19, I suffered a manic episode, or a period of extremely high energy to the point where I was not sleeping for days, and I was hospitalized at a hospital on my college campus. After ruling out drugs or brain damage, they diagnosed me with bipolar disorder type I. I stayed in this hospital for two and a half weeks before going back to my hometown for a medical leave of absence. At this point, I had to find a doctor to treat me at home.

My parents are divorced, and they engaged in a lot of conflict throughout our family's history. While it was often very painful to watch my parents present dueling ideas, in this case their competition changed my life because my mom and dad each found me a different doctor. My father found a referral from one of his friends to a highly specialized doctor called a neuropsychopharmacologist. I saw this man first. He was extremely clinical and robotic. He told me that my brain had suffered brain damage from what would be the equivalent of a lot of drinking over a long period of time. He called this cell death "neural apoptosis." He said that I needed a complex cocktail of medications and that I would have to take a full year away from college to recover, while doing very minimal activities.

Next, I met my mother's doctor referral. He was a psychiatrist. He told me I could take just a semester off of school, and if all went well, we could try monotherapy—a single drug instead of a cocktail.

Realizing that I had a choice about my care, I chose the second doctor. His treatment plan was not a definitive right answer, but it was the right answer for me based on my personal perspective (again, my perspective is biased, even in how I recall these two clinicians now). Others may have preferred the more rigorous clinician who had been running academic studies on the subject, and they might have opted for his increased treatment regimen. The point of this story is not to tell you I made the right choice; rather, I want you to understand that I had a choice.

This was the first big choice I made to take care of my mental health. It is a choice many people do not realize they have because many just follow a single path without realizing multiple options are available. And these were options that I only saw because my parents are divorced. This choice was only the beginning. Every day, a person makes countless decisions about their mental health. For me, any moment could be the moment I choose to do more research about my condition or opt to switch clinicians or ask my current clinician for something different. The takeaway is that these are all personal decisions without definitive right answers.

iv. Workplace Case Study: Company Mental Health Decisions

A common refrain from managers looking to improve their mental health communication and conflict resolution practices at work is that they wish they had known about an employee's mental health problems sooner. Whether a manager ends up cutting them some slack informally or whether they end up going for a formal disability accommodation following human resources procedures, many bosses are disappointed that the disclosure of a mental health condition came too late to prevent problems that occurred at work—missed deadlines, low-quality work, interpersonal conflicts, and so on.

Similarly, many managers also complain about people who have never taken advantage of the company's employee assistance plan (EAP). This common service offers limited mental health benefits to support employees through difficult life transitions and other mental health problems. "Why did we invest all of this money into the EAP, only to have it utilized by less than 10% of staff?" "Why are people living with these mental health problems if they could easily use the health insurance and EAPs we provide to get treatment?"

In chapter 8, we discuss how to promote mental health resources in a broad, universal manner that does not single anyone out or pressure anyone to make a specific choice such as disclosing their mental health problem or utilizing a company's EAP. For now, it is important to note that these statements are inadvertently paternalistic because they presume someone *ought* to tell us early instead of respecting their rights to privacy, and because it is their personal choice to disclose or not to disclose at any time. While these are common reactions to frustrations about challenges at work, they are not grounded in respect for each person's right to manage their own affairs. The solution to the manager's frustration is to develop better policies for responding to challenging workplace behaviors without invading anyone's privacy about their mental health. We share tools for developing behavior-based approaches in chapter 9.

Similarly, we need to recognize that, although a company may invest in mental health benefits as an option for their employees, employees do not have to choose to use those benefits. Think of it like a company that offers an in-house daycare program. Does the existence of such a program mean that employees cannot choose to invest in a different daycare service that is not at work? What if they choose to hire help at home, or what if their partner or a relative or a friend stays home with the child? Does having a daycare service on site mean it's your business's right to know what every employee decides to do with their own children? Chapter 8 helps orient us to the philosophy that our universal offerings of help such as the EAP do not mean we can expect anyone to take advantage of the services or even disclose what they are doing. While it is great to offer helpful options, we must always remember it is outside our role to require lifestyle changes or to monitor them.

Mental health choices are decisions like any other choices. Chapter 3 discusses some of the roles that stigma, assumptions, and paternalism play in guiding our minds to places they do not belong—places of assuming we know what might be best for someone else, rather than respecting their autonomy. It is certainly well meaning to offer support, but we must remember that these offers do not entitle us to invade someone's privacy or compel them to make different choices.

TAKEAWAY

Remember that mental health is a world filled with options and choices, as opposed to definitive answers. If you offer options, respect that a person may not take advantage of them on your timeline if they ever do at all.

E. MENTAL HEALTH EXPERIENCES

We have discussed different perspectives of mental health and mental illness, as well as the wide variety of choices people have about how to manage their mental health needs. It stands to reason, then, that everyone's experience of mental health is unique to them.

This section provides an overview of how experiences may differ, as well as some examples of the kinds of experiences people have. Remember that, while this section shares some insights that can help you become sensitive to the wide variety of different experiences associated with mental health, it is always important not to generalize any of these experiences to anyone. Rather, be aware that anyone, anywhere, may have experienced something like what we cover in this section.

i. Why Experiences May Vary

There are many reasons explaining why different people have different experiences regarding mental health needs. The first reason is their role. There are many different roles in the world of mental health. For instance, someone can be a person with their own lived experience of a mental health problem; a supporter of someone who lives with a mental illness; a mental health professional; or all of the above. Within these broad categories a person can have many other types of roles, and these roles will be one of many factors contributing to a person's experiences.

Another factor is their cultural background. Mental health views can be influenced by a variety of cultures, including those based on country, religion, ethnicity, workplace, or family, to name a few. Just as is true of roles, there are many different types of subcultures, and each person lives within their own unique interplay of cultures that impact their mental health experiences.

People are also influenced by the clinicians and services they visit. They have access to a wide variety of mental health professionals, therapies, and services, all of which help shape their perspectives. Likewise, one can get involved in many different mental health communities, which will also impact their experiences. A wide variety of different advocacy organizations, support groups, and other communities may share their particular views with people.

Experiences can also be different based on a person's beliefs about the causes, labels, and treatment that are appropriate for times of instability. These beliefs will guide different people toward different choices that can ripple out into different life experiences.

Each person's path is different based on how they encounter the mental health system. Individuals have personal lived experiences that may include difficult times, coping experiences, support system relationships, side effects, trauma, and other impactful events.

Finally, the language people use can affect their experiences. Whatever terminologies people use to identify themselves, describe their lived experience of mental health, and explain tough times will have an impact on the ways they are treated and the experiences they have.

TAKEAWAY

People have unique, complex backgrounds, including their roles, cultures, and experiences surrounding mental health. These nuances help explain why many people have different mental health experiences and why it is important we validate any experiences anyone shares rather than assuming there are any "right" answers for them.

ii. Some Examples of Mental Health Experiences

People can have many different kinds of experiences related to their mental health. It is important never to pry about someone's experiences or make assumptions about them. However, it is also helpful to be aware of some of the challenging things people may experience related to mental health needs.

This section introduces a few of these challenges in a very quick and superficial way, simply to give you a general sense of what kinds of things may be related to mental health. Do not make any assumptions that any specific person has experienced any of these things but remain conscious that anyone you encounter may have experienced some of them.

Some types of mental health experiences include:

- *Symptoms:* Examples may include anxiety, delusions, hallucinations, depression, sensitivity to noise, confusion, and the inability to concentrate.

- *Side Effects:* Examples may include weight gain, acne, diarrhea, tremors, facial tic, headache, dehydration, and vivid nightmares.

- *Hospitalization:* During hospitalization, a person may experience intense supervision/behavior logging, heavy medication with minimal therapy, involuntary interventions, and decreased agency.

- *Forced Treatment:* This treatment could be in the form of just pressure to take medication or it could involve commitment and even restraints. It may also involve the person feeling pressured or the person feeling completely dismissed, with their perspective being seen as totally invalid given their mental illness.

- *Life Interruptions and Lost Relationships:* Many people with mental health problems may take longer to achieve life milestones because the time spent addressing their condition delays them. They also can lose relationships along the way due to those delays, stigma, or events related to their illness.

- *Treatment Challenges:* These may include resource shortages, inability to afford care, problems finding the right fit, confusion navigating different medical opinions, or the disappointing reality that treatment does not always work.

- *Sense of Self:* People may spend time questioning which of their choices and life events are the product of their personality and which are due to their "disorder." They may struggle with the decision to seek support, and they may feel insecurity regarding their capabilities.

- *Social Fit:* People dealing with mental health problems may have to cope with changing expectations from their loved ones, being dismissed as ill, and being treated paternalistically

Those supporting a loved one may experience a number of particular experiences such as the following:

- *Direct Trauma:* Supporters may experience direct trauma from being with their loved one during the symptoms, side effects, hospitalizations, and related problems, as well as from talking about it.

- *Limited Information:* Supporters may have limited information about how their loved one is doing because of confidentiality laws protecting clinicians from sharing their records. They also often must rely on their loved one to give them snippets about how they are doing whereas their loved one experiencing the mental health problems has full self-knowledge of their own thoughts, feelings, and experiences.

- *Shortage of Resources:* Supporters may have to struggle to conduct research, find treatment professionals, and schedule them for their loved ones. They may also be affected by the shortage of resources in the world of mental health.

- *Confusion Regarding Expectations:* It can be hard to decide whether to push someone to get back to their normal life so that they can thrive (but assume the risk of their becoming overstressed and having problems again) versus whether to protect them and be gentler (but assume the risk of their becoming infantilized or stunted).

- *Feeling Responsible:* Supporters may feel responsible for their loved one's problems because of the things they did not do (e.g., "I should have caught this problem earlier"), because of the things they did do (e.g., "I shouldn't have pushed my loved one so hard!"), and—if it's a family member—because of their genetic history, which might play a role in their loved one's vulnerability.

Mental health treatment providers have some of their own perspectives and experiences too, such as the following:

- *Seeing Through a Professional Lens:* Providers may ask questions, interpret behaviors, and provide recommendations based on their training and the norms of their specific profession.

- *Managing Multiple Cases:* Providers may not be as immersed in any one case as a peer or supporter might be because they see the case in the context of a larger caseload; they may have time constraints for this reason; or they may form insights from the patterns they personally experience across cases.

- ■ *Navigating a Shortage of Resources:* Providers may also have to struggle with the shortage of resources for their clients, particularly if they are trying to refer them to support services.

- ■ *Developing Expectations from Past Clients:* Providers may form expectations based on their past clients. For instance, if they lost someone due to suicide or struggled supporting one of their past clients, they could have a traumatic reaction and they could become more risk averse. Generally speaking, providers tend to see people at their worst, so that could also color their expectations. (Typically, people make appointments with providers because they are struggling, and during those sessions they tend to share the most upsetting things in their lives, so this could skew provider impressions.)

TAKEAWAY

Everyone you encounter has their own experiences that inform who they are and what choices they make. Some may have experienced trauma. These experiences are theirs to decide to share or keep private. We must always maintain an awareness that anyone could be impacted by any kind of positive or negative experience, that this may inform their behaviors, and that their experiences and choices are valid for them.

iii. Some Examples of Mental Health Terminologies

People use many different words for different mental health experiences, and they use these words differently, so it is important to always keep an open mind and ask what they mean. Mental health stakeholders have differing perceptions of the appropriate way to denote a mental health problem. The vernacular ranges from *patient* among many medical professionals to *consumer, peer, survivor, user of services, person with a psychiatric history,* and many other terms.[33] The biomedical model, supported by the DSM-5, has dominated the way many stakeholders conceptualize mental health problems, in large part due to the heavy influence of pharmaceutical companies in shaping the national conversation about mental health.[34,35] This dynamic has proliferated the language of "mental disorder" and specific conditions. Recently, the head of the American Psychiatric Association (APA) spoke out against use of the term *mentally ill.*[36] These linguistic debates have triggered sensitivities across different mental health

---

[33] IAPSRS Language Policy Task Force. (2003). IAPSRS language guidelines. *PSR Canneaimz, Summer,* 1–9.

[34] Read, J., & Cain, A. (2013). A literature review and meta-analysis of drug company-funded mental health websites. *Acta Psychiatrica Scandinavica, 128*(6), 422–433.

[35] Barker, P., & Buchanan-Barker, P. (2012). First, do no harm: Confronting the myths of psychiatric drugs. *Nursing Ethics, 19*(4), 451–463.

[36] Golberberg, C. (2014). A phrase to renounce for 2014: "The Mentally Ill." WBUR. Retrieved from https://www.wbur.org/news/2014/01/03/renounce-term-the-mentally-ill.

communities. They underscore the potential for conflict resolution professionals to enrich conversation through their time-tested processes and strong communication skills.

The key theme for conflict resolvers is to not assume we know what someone means by terms that may be more ambiguous than we realize. Instead, we must listen closely and ask questions to appreciate what people are trying to convey with the language they are using. That said, here are some terms that are often used to describe people living with mental health problems. They are presented so you can familiarize yourself with them so you know that there may be more to these words than you realize when you hear them.

- **Patient:** Doctors often call the people who visit them patients, and patient is a common term clinicians use that normally does not cause offense.[37] At the same time, this term is often seen as stigmatizing in the world of mental health because of the negative slur of the "mental patient" as used in sensationalist media portrayals.[38]

- **Recipient, Client, User:** The terms *recipient, client,* and *user* evolved as a way to indicate someone who is in the community of people living with mental health problems without defining them as a patient (which had often been seen as having paternalistic connotations). The idea behind use of these terms is to empower people.

- **Consumer/Survivor:** Self-advocacy groups started the consumer and survivor movements around 1970 in response to the need for new ways of thinking about patient's rights and the idea that people who actually had experienced mental health problems may possess valuable insights.[39] These terms are still used often today, but with many degrees of differences within their own subcultures as well as overlaps with other usages of these common words. For instance, the word "survivor" does not have to mean that someone survived an abusive and paternalistic mental health system. It could signal the person believes they survived their condition or a suicide attempt.

- **Peer:** Normally, a peer is anyone who can relate to the shared experience of another—in other words, people in the same group. Because of the rich history of peer support programs in mental health, many people have come to use the term *peer* to designate that they are someone with lived experience of a mental health problem. This is becoming increasingly codified as professional peer worker roles have been created, such as the role of the peer specialist—trained workers with lived mental health experience who function on treatment teams, providing support and often serving as a positive role model of living successfully with a mental health condition. Most states now have some kind of accreditation for this kind of worker, and their services are insurance-reimbursable. This is an indication that the idea of "peer" is here to

---

[37] Costa, D. S., Mercieca-Bebber, R., Tesson, S., Seidler, Z., & Lopez, A. L. (2019). Patient, client, consumer, survivor or other alternatives? A scoping review of preferred terms for labelling individuals who access healthcare across settings. *BMJ Open, 9*(3), 1–16.

[38] Klin, A., & Lemish, D. (2008). Mental disorders stigma in the media: Review of studies on production, content, and influences. *Journal of Health Communication, 13*(5), 434–449.

[39] Tomes, N. (2006). The patient as a policy factor: A historical case study of the consumer/survivor movement in mental health. *Health Affairs, 25*(3), 720–729.

stay.[40] As with other terms, it is important to ask people what they mean when they use the term.

Below are different words people may use to describe living with a mental health problem:

- **Recovery:** This term is sometimes used differently in mental health contexts than in its conventional understanding as being completely better from an illness. Given that mental health problems can be chronic and lifelong, recovery is often defined as finding an equilibrium of coping skills that allow for a high quality of life. Because quality of life is a subjective outcome, sometimes this term can be used paternalistically (e.g., an expert or family member telling someone that, for their recovery, they can only handle part-time work when they would rather have full employment). Indeed, certain coping skills deficits and internalized stigma are correlated with worse recovery outcomes.[41]

- **Sick, Breakdown, and Tough Time:** When I speak to my family and I say, "I'm worried I am getting sick," they know that for me that means I have anxiety about my experience of potential mental health symptoms that could indicate I am at risk for a bipolar episode. Most people, however, tend to mean physical health conditions when they use the word "sick." The same logic applies to terms like "breakdown" or "tough time." These words can mean different things to different people and across different contexts.

- **Episode:** The term *episode* can mean many things, and it often can connote the medical idea of a discrete episode—a manic episode, bipolar episode, panic attack, and so on. If someone says they had experienced a "difficult episode" or anything in that realm, it could be their attempt to communicate about their mental health. As with all other terms, it is important to confirm the person's meaning rather than make our own assumptions.

TAKEAWAY

A lot of different mental health terminologies mean different things to different people. Ask people what they mean rather than make assumptions.

---

[40] Kaufman, L., Brooks, W., Bellinger, J., Steinley-Bumgarner, M., & Stevens-Manser, S. (2014). Peer specialist training and certification programs: A national overview. Texas Institute for Excellence in Mental Health, School of Social Work, University of Texas at Austin.

[41] Chronister, J., Chou, C. C., & Liao, H. Y. (2013). The role of stigma coping and social support in mediating the effect of societal stigma on internalized stigma, mental health recovery, and quality of life among people with serious mental illness. *Journal of Community Psychology, 41*(5), 582–600.

F. FAMILY CASE STUDY: CONVINCING LOVED ONES TO BELIEVE THEY'RE ILL

Families seeking help in resolving conflicts often come into a mediation debating the existence of a mental health problem, the "correct" diagnosis, and the "right" form of treatment to pursue. Human beings like arriving at answers and solutions, but conflict professionals appreciate that life is often more nuanced than that.

There is never a single right outcome for a conflict—each party arrives with their own point of view, and each party has their own set of choices that they can make. Together, the parties will hopefully reach a sustainable, realistic agreement to resolve their conflict, but there is no such thing as a perfect or correct one. In the end, people work together to make the right decisions for them in that moment.

As we have seen in this chapter, self-determination is especially important when we are approaching mental health choices. A number of robust academic, scientific fields devote considerable study to mental disorders so they can make recommendations about diagnostic criteria for diagnosing a mental health problem and best practices to treat them. However, there are no definitive right answers in mental health. The field is very young, the diagnostic criteria can be subjective and evolving, and the treatment recommendations are diverse. There are many complementary and alternative approaches to mental health treatment that are scoffed at before they become codified as vital aspects to care, such as mindfulness meditation or medicine-free interventions for schizophrenia. Even when there is clear expert consensus as to the best diagnosis and treatment options for a particular person, it is still up to that person to choose how they want to live their life. There are a number of reasons they may decide not to agree with a label or to avoid a certain treatment, including cultural beliefs, side effects, and many others.

Yet family members are often not open-minded to their loved ones' alternative views. Many families end up in conflicts trying to convince one another that certain beliefs are correct or certain options are the only appropriate option.

This case study focuses on one of two parents who were in conflict with their 20-year-old daughter, who had been previously diagnosed with bipolar disorder. The parents were upset because their daughter was living with them and had begun smoking in the house. Normally, she would smoke outside in accordance with family rules. They interpreted her smoking inside the home as a sign that her mental health was deteriorating, and they started insisting she "take her medication."

Many professional mediators might assume that the mere presence of a mental illness diagnosis, or the suggestion that she was not taking medication as prescribed, could be red flags necessitating special treatment. Some mediation programs might even inappropriately screen out the case for these reasons. However, neither of those responses are appropriate because both would be based on perceptions about mental health instead of objective behavior-based standards.

Instead, the best practices are to develop specific behavioral criteria with which to make decisions about when it is appropriate to make process adjustments, terminate the conflict, or treat the situation as a health emergency. All parties in a conflict should be treated the same, with the understanding that it is inappropriate to judge someone's choice to believe in a diagnostic label or their decision to decline a medication.

So, what happened to our family in the case described above? In my practice we do not ever mediate disputes about peoples' beliefs about mental health, but we support everyone's right to form their own beliefs and to make their own choices. Through this kind of brief dialogue about the boundaries of the conflict resolution process, we end up setting aside the nonproductive, repetitive arguments where one person insists the other has an illness and the other insists they do not, or one person insists the other needs medicine and the other that they do not. Instead, we get down to the choices everybody has in this particular conflict.

In this case, we moved away from a discussion about whether or not the daughter was sick or needed medicine, and we began talking about how to address the actual conflict being discussed—the rules of the house. In other words, can we reach an agreement about smoking outside of the house? Shifting the conversation in this manner not only got us past the paternalism being linked to the mental health labeling, but it also became an opportunity for the family to communicate about why this smoking problem was happening instead of acting on assumptions.

There is also always a chance, in working through the obstacles about smoking inside versus outside, that we will segue into a conversation about the daughter's possible challenges managing to smoke outside and that the daughter, on her own, could start sharing her feelings about the barriers she experiences due to her mental health problem. She may even open up about her own internal confusion about whether it is a mental health problem, whether she feels safe with the medication, and whether she trusts telling her parents she is feeling vulnerable. This would be an empowering way for the mental health topic to come up—on her terms, in response to discussions about behaviors instead of judgments about mental health.

The key to shifting to conversations like this one is to embrace the idea that everyone has choices, and following the lead of those choices rather than getting lost in trying to convince every family member to believe the same thing. Some people are skeptical of this approach. They say that if we see that someone has a mental health problem, then we must do something special to help them. Chapter 5 talks about this idea of whether people need help and makes the clear case that this kind of thinking is paternalistic and unnecessary. Chapters 8 and 9 provide a way to offer help and respond to problems without ever going down the dangerous road of making assumptions about someone's mental health.

TAKEAWAY

Fighting to convince someone to change their beliefs can be stigmatizing and counterproductive, while framing a conversation around their choices may lead everyone toward more fruitful, empowering discussions and agreements.

G. WORKPLACE CASE STUDY: IDENTIFYING MENTAL HEALTH ISSUES AT WORK

Many training programs teach managers, school faculty, or others to recognize potential signs of different disorders so that they can step in and intervene. An example training program is Mental Health First Aid (MHFA), which provides a brief introduction to a few mental health conditions, coupled with a framework that helps bystanders understand how to assess someone's risk for mental instability, listen to them, and share information and resource referrals.[42] At one point, I was briefly an MHFA trainer with the New York City Department of Health and Mental Hygiene, so I am familiar with this program. I have watched, with great interest, as it has proliferated across a wide variety of organizations as a way to prepare people for supporting coworkers and clients who may have mental health needs.

These kinds of training programs are very common, yet they are also risky. While it can be helpful for people to have this information and to learn ways to offer help to colleagues in distress, it can also be dangerous. As we've discussed, it is generally not our place to make a determination about someone else's mental health. It is a dangerous thing to do because it is rooted in our own biases, it is inherently paternalistic, and it can inadvertently amount to discrimination.

Many people informally tell their peers at work that they know what they are going through. Perhaps they recognize the signs they were taught to see in training, or they have personal experiences that help them understand—or maybe they, too, live with mental health problems or they have a loved one who does. While people who offer this kind of understanding and support are well intentioned, they are also accidentally making a lot of assumptions about the other person's mental health. Just because we have training, experience supporting a loved one, or our own mental health history does not mean we are in a good position to understand someone else's. To understand another person's point of view, we need to step away from all of these personal biases and focus on listening to them.

Mental health training is often disempowering because it teaches people to form new biases and recognize signs. This book suggests a better way to discuss mental health needs at work by becoming universally accessible. Those workplaces and managers that do want to generously and kindly offer mental health resources can still do so, but they ought to do it without singling anyone out and assessing individuals for signs of mental health conditions.

Managers and colleagues can comment on challenging behaviors they notice at work—absences, missed deadlines, lower quality work, or interpersonal conflicts—without making the leap to connecting those behaviors to potential mental health problems. Just as we learned with the family case study, it is best to have an open-minded conversation about these behaviors instead of getting sidetracked into a conversation about someone's mental health. Especially in the workplace context, those kinds of detours can be hazardous because the ADA places strict limits on the types of health inquiries that are allowed at work. It prohibits treating someone differently even if they are merely regarded as potentially having a psychiatric disability, regardless of whether they actually do have one.[43]

If a company chooses to provide mental health resources, chapter 8 discusses ways to promote company programs without making any guesses about who may have a mental health problem. Providing support resources in this universal manner is appropriate in a workplace or in virtually any other setting. Chapter 9 shares resources for addressing challenging behaviors without linking them to assumptions or inquiries about mental health.

---

[42] Kitchener, B. A., & Jorm, A. F. (2006). Mental health first aid training: Review of evaluation studies. *Australian and New Zealand Journal of Psychiatry, 40*(1), 6–8.

[43] Bagenstos, S. R. (2017). The EEOC, the ADA, and workplace wellness programs. *Health Matrix, 27*, 81.

TAKEAWAY

Learning about mental disorders and mental health experiences can be dangerous if it leads you to form new biases and to act on these assumptions. You can never know what someone else is experiencing. Instead, focus on each person's choices and listen to what they share about their perspective and their history. Offer support universally without profiling based on mental health and respond to observed behaviors rather than guessing connections to mental health.

H. MENTAL HEALTH PERSPECTIVE SCENARIOS

Roles: *Consumer, Survivor, Family Member, Psychiatrist, Psychologist, Layperson*

Think about who among these roles might say each of the following statements:

1. I have a hard time figuring out what behaviors are due to mental illness.

2. Drug side-effects can ruin someone's life.

3. I am worried that there may be another episode of mental instability.

4. I don't understand the concept of mental illness.

5. I think that mental illness is a purely biological condition that someone can't control without medication.

6. I think mental illness is caused by environmental triggers.

7. Psychiatrists know what they are doing and are the best place to get good mental health treatment.

As you go through this exercise, ask yourself the following questions:

- What assumptions are you making about a person in this perspective category? How might they be wrong?

- Why do you believe a person in this role would say this statement? Who else might ever say this statement, and why?

- How sure are you in your understanding of what the person means by this statement? What questions might you ask them to better understand them? What questions might feel inappropriate to ask?

I. VALIDATE ALL MENTAL HEALTH PERSPECTIVES TIPSHEET (TOOL)

Validating means respecting someone's right to form their own point of view, even if you do not necessarily agree with it. In conflict resolution practices, we make sure everyone feels validated, and we strive to validate different perspectives equally. This tipsheet provides reminders that can help you stay focused on validating different mental health perspectives:

▶ **Mental Health Issues Are Highly Prevalent but Manifest Uniquely**

According to the National Institute of Mental Health, one in five American adults experience a diagnosable mental disorder each year, with close to one in two experiencing a mental health problem during their lifetime. Moreover, we all have mental health needs from time to time even if they do not rise to the level of a diagnosable problem. Everyone experiences their mental health situations in their own unique ways, based on their values, beliefs, and culture.

▶ **Validate Unconventional Choices**

There are no perfect answers in mental health, and people can rationally reach unconventional choices. Many people don't respond to treatment, and many others have debilitating side effects that lead them to halt it. "Alternative" approaches to treatment that may seem unconventional can become mainstream and evidence-based, such as mindfulness approaches.

▶ **Ask People What Language They Prefer**

Different people identify with different communities and different terminologies. When talking about mental health, ask people what they mean by different terms and what terms they prefer.

▶ **Mental Health Is Often a Long, Complicated Journey**

Often people feel a desire to try to solve someone's mental health problem and find the perfect resource right away. While some people do find solutions very quickly, for many it is a long and difficult journey. Instead of focusing on solutions, it is crucial to meet someone where they are at and to respect their choices.

▶ **How Someone Is on a Bad Day Does Not Define Who They Are**

Often people in helping roles have a negative bias because they typically see people during crises and problems. You might be getting the worst possible impression of a person because you are there on the toughest days. Remember that where they are at today does not define who they are.

▶ **Mental Health Is Sensitive**

People may have had intense experiences around mental health, so they may be sensitive about discussing it. Anyone may have had a history of trauma or mental health problems. It is important to be sensitive and open-minded with everyone.

J. VALIDATING DIVERSE MENTAL HEALTH PERSPECTIVES CHECKLIST (TOOL)

Validating perspectives is important because it helps the person feel heard, helps remind you there are no "right" answers (only choices), and helps you appreciate their perspective.

If you want to be impartial and open-minded about diverse mental health experiences, you can use the accompanying checklist to check-in with yourself about how well you are doing. No one can ever do a perfect job, so please remember that this checklist is aspirational. Use it to set goals, not to criticize yourself.

Are you:

☐ Equally respectful to people who call themselves patients, peers, consumers, survivors, or users? Or to people who do not feel their sensitivities are an illness?

☐ Able to support someone who has chosen an alternative way of addressing their mental health situation just as much as you support someone who is following the exact advice of a medical clinician?

☐ Aware that mental health professionals, family members, and people living with mental health issues may have different perspectives on a situation and are you able to validate all points of view?

☐ Able to not form a judgment when someone talks to you about their mental health situation?

☐ Able to not give your opinion when someone talks to you about their mental health situation?

☐ Accepting of a mental health situation without trying to fix it?

☐ Supportive to anyone who talks to you about mental health regardless of whether you agree with their perspective?

☐ Disregarding any assumptions you are making about their mental health?

Don't Negate; Elaborate

You can validate someone's perspective while sharing new information by explaining it as additional information rather than telling the person they are wrong. Take the "Yes, and . . ." approach.

CHAPTER 2

HOW DO MENTAL HEALTH CONCERNS COME UP IN DISPUTES?

So far we've learned enough about mental health and mental illness to know that it's best to keep an open mind rather than trust our own ideas and assumptions. This chapter explores the different times the topic may arise.

Broadly speaking, there are four circumstances when someone's mental health concerns become salient during a conflict: when we already know, when someone tells us, when there are accusations, and when we suspect.

A. When We Already Know

Sometimes, it is known that a mental health concern is present in a situation. It is important to pay attention to how we know this information and to stop ourselves from making assumptions. We may be aware of a mental health concern due to a variety of ways, including the following:

> ▶ **It is part of the facts of the case.**

One example is an employment discrimination case where the dispute is about a person alleging they experienced disparate treatment because an employer knew of their mental health condition. Other examples are a special education mediation where the dispute is about providing additional services for someone with a diagnosis, or a custody dispute where the mental health problem is being seen as a factor.

> ▶ **It has been known for a long time.**

This might be the case if the people in the conflict have a history and therefore were aware of one another's mental health histories before the conflict arose. It may also be the case in a workplace setting where a manager or human resources professional is aware of the mental health history as part of a reasonable accommodation process at that job.

> ▶ **It is public record**

This manner of knowing applies to me all of the time because anyone who Googles me can see my TEDxTalk or other trainings and read that I have bipolar disorder. Learning about the condition based on someone publicly having disclosed it is different from learning about it through direct disclosure. The key difference is that you may have some information about this condition, but the person has not indicated they would like to talk with you about it. It is important, then, to avoid assuming that just because you now are aware of the mental health condition that it is incumbent on you to ask the person about it. Instead, continue your same process as you would with anyone in conflict. For instance, a professional conflict resolver should not ask me if I need any special assistance based on knowing my mental health condition. Rather, they would be better served asking all parties if they would like process adjustments equally, as part of their standard practices. We will further discuss this universal design approach in chapter 8.

It may be that you have already decided to be supportive of all people's potential mental health needs, as we will cover in chapter 8, or you may react to challenging behaviors in a certain way, as we will explore in chapter 9. Yet those decisions need to be based on your general practices, not on the information you know about the person's mental health condition. Moreover, remember that all the information you receive is inherently subjective, so do not assume you know the full story about that person's mental health even if you are seeing it written up as objective data, such as stipulated as part of the facts for a case.

TAKEAWAY

If mental health information is already known but you were not given it directly, it is important that you do not factor that into your decision-making about offering process adjustments or addressing challenging behaviors. Also, do not ask about the condition just because you have learned about it. Lastly, do not assume your information is correct.

i. Workplace Case Study: Assuming What "Bipolar" Means

During a mental health communication training I delivered for a university, I shared the lesson that we ask people what they mean even if they disclose a diagnosis which we know a lot about. For instance, if I tell you "I have bipolar disorder," it is important to ask me what I want you to glean from that rather than assuming you know what I mean.

The director of counseling services, an esteemed mental health professional, bristled at this suggestion. She explained that of course she was trained to know and understand what it means if someone has bipolar disorder, and she absolutely would not need to ask what I meant if I told her.

I asked her some quick questions to illustrate some of the information she might be missing:

- Do you know if this person is suffering from bipolar disorder type I, bipolar disorder type II, or some other type? Many different clinical diagnoses are possible under the category of "bipolar disorder."

- Do you know if the person has problems with elevated moods, depressed moods, or some combination? Are they persisting a long time in protracted episodes? Do they fluctuate often, rapid cycling? Are they happening now or are they euthymic (i.e., experiencing stable mood) now?

- Assuming they are experiencing depression symptoms, do you know if the person is dealing with the type of depression where they sleep too much or the kind where they sleep too little? Might they be eating too much or too little? All of these are possible symptoms, and every person has a unique way of experiencing them.

- Are they actively going through something now? Do they need help? Do they want help from you?

- Do they agree with the diagnosis or not? Do they agree with mainstream treatment or not? If so, do they believe in medication, talk therapy, or some kind of mixture? Are they happy with their doctor? Is their diagnosis longstanding or new? Does every doctor they consult agree with it? Are there other diagnoses too?

The counseling director conceded that she had no way of knowing what the person wanted her to know about their mental health condition. She also acknowledged that asking that question would be a great way to see what they cared about rather than holding onto our own assumptions about the person's mental health. It also would save us the trouble of asking this endless stream of questions to validate our own guesses about what might be going on.

Mental health professionals may know more about these kinds of conditions, and they may feel confident that their perspective delivers some right answers about what these labels mean. Even so, we must listen to people to learn what their choices are and what they've decided the best answers are for them. Perhaps more importantly, we have to listen to people to know what they are looking for from us.

This idea of making someone feel heard and respecting their choices is a crucial foundation for all conflict resolution best practices. But when mental health concerns are involved, it is essential for another reason—to avoid inadvertent discrimination. We will continue this discussion in Part II. Suffice it to say here, assuming someone needs something based on knowing their mental health condition is, on some level, inherently discriminatory. The proper way to offer help is to give them an opportunity to share what they need, on their terms, and delivering them help when they ask for it. We can also offer help to everyone in an accessible way, as we will cover in chapter 8.

TAKEAWAY

Even when you believe you are aware of a mental health situation, your interpretations are not the full story. Keep an open mind rather than making assumptions.

ii. Family Case Study: Living Together Amidst a New Diagnosis

Ray and Sam are frustrated with their adult son, Ralph. Ralph is in his twenties and has been home from college on medical leave for his first bout of what his doctor diagnosed as major depression.

Ray and Sam have done their best to be supportive to Ralph, but Ralph is not following the rules of the house even though he used to be very diligent with them before his mental health episode.

Sam has asked Ralph to please leave his shoes by the door instead of strewn around the house and to pick up after himself when he eats. Ralph has been very irritable and mouths off to Sam whenever she points out that she has noticed that Ralph is not following what she calls these "simple" house rules.

Sam is not sure what to do about what's happening. Ralph is keeping all of the information about his visits to his doctors private because that is his right. Therefore, Sam is not able to talk to the doctor to find out if Ralph is able to handle cleaning up after himself or if he is too limited from the depression. From Sam's perspective, it is important to find the answers to her questions because she wants to be supportive of Ralph if he is struggling, but she does not want to be taken advantage of.

Ray, on the other hand, does not want to hear from the doctor at all. She grew up in a family that believes there is no such thing as mental health or mental illness. To them, people are just productive or they are lazy. Although she understands that Ralph is suffering, she is still not really on board with the mental health lingo; she just wants to hold Ralph accountable for his behavior.

How are they to navigate these problems? Many families would start the conversation by asking Ralph about his depression and his appointments with his doctor. This is potentially a viable path for conflict resolution. Indeed, many people do decide to waive their privacy rights and share their confidential medical information with loved ones after they come to understand why that information may be of value to them. (Many others, incidentally, want to share that information with their family or support system all on their own.)

However, it is treacherous to bring up any questions about someone's mental health if they do not bring it up first themselves. In this situation, the best starting point is to focus on the household behaviors. Remember we begin each situation by looking at our role, and here their roles are that they are living in the same household. Asking about household behaviors is not as inflammatory or invasive as asking about Ralph's mental health.

This conversation would treat Ralph as one would address anyone else discussing household dynamics, without highlighting the mental health concerns. The discussion may then expand into a conversation about Ralph's mental health situation if he decides to share it. Perhaps he will say that he feels people are looking at him differently because of the major depression diagnosis. Perhaps he will say he is limited in what's possible for him to do because of that condition. Or perhaps he will say nothing about it. These are his choices related to his mental health experiences.

Ray and Sam cannot push to discuss the condition without being disempowering, but they do have standing to talk about the household behaviors. That conversation should become the backbone of any discussions, even if it ends up eventually becoming an empowering conversation about mental health once Ralph is ready to talk about it.

The most important thing to notice about this situation is that everyone's awareness of the mental health history makes it harder to hold a simple open-ended conversation about how everyone can respect boundaries in the household. There is a natural gravity that pulls people into fixating on mental health diagnoses and concerns when that does not have to be the center of the conversation. When we push to go there, the effect may be to derail the conversation. Be aware that your knowledge of a mental health problem may steer you in this nonproductive, disempowering direction.

TAKEAWAY

Focus on the behaviors that are related to your role in the situation, instead of bringing up the person's mental health situation. That behavior conversation could expand to include that person's mental health needs if they bring them up, but it doesn't have to. We should never aim to have that mental health conversation: it is the other person's decision whether they would like to have it or not.

B. WHEN SOMEONE TELLS US

Sometimes, mental health concerns arise because someone shares their situation. As we have already discussed, it is vital to listen to the person and ask them what they want you to know from their disclosure. This is how you can guide your response.

Later, in chapter 8, we will talk about how to develop accessible practices so that you can offer help to everyone without relying on your own assumptions about mental health needs. We will also explore how to respond to disclosures that amount to requests for help.

Yet it is always vital to understand that a disclosure is not always a sign that a person is asking for help. Here are some ways someone can disclose a mental illness without asking for help:

- Someone casually mentions their mental illness because it is not a big deal to them.

- Someone is proud of their self-care efforts, and they disclose their mental illness as part of feeling good about their recovery journey.

- Someone is describing a difficulty they are presently experiencing in their life, but they do not want your help with it.

- Someone is remembering something from a long time ago, and they place the timeline by referencing something that happened around the same time and was related to their mental illness.

- Someone is nervous that their mental illness is going to be outed by the person they are in conflict with, and they decide to share their mental illness proactively.

- Someone tells a joke about mental health and assures you they feel it is okay to do so because they have a mental illness themselves.

These are just some of the many ways a person may mention a mental health problem without asking for any help. In that case, it is important for you not to start talking to them as if they need help, but instead to continue following your universal practices for offering support to anyone. We will explore more in depth about how to create these practices in chapter 8.

What if the person wants help? Well, depending on your role, you may be legally obligated to provide what is called a "reasonable accommodation" to adjust your processes. The ADA creates that responsibility, and it affects different entities in different ways. However, there are some clear guidelines of what amounts to such a request. The general rule is that a request for a reasonable accommodation may be happening any time someone asks for help while linking the request to a potential medical need.[44]

For now, let's just appreciate the fact that there is a distinction between someone telling you about their mental health condition because they want help and telling you for some other reason. These are two very different categories of disclosure. In either case, we are going to learn ways to make sure people are able to get whatever support they are entitled to without inadvertently singling them out in ways that could amount to discrimination.

TAKEAWAY

People disclose their mental health conditions for all sorts of reasons. Stay mindful that sharing a mental health problem does not in itself amount to a request for help and that assuming it does can lead to inadvertent paternalism and discrimination.

i. Personal Story: A Referral to a Mediation Center

People often reach out to me, looking for guidance when they encounter a person with a mental illness as part of their cases. This is the story of a case manager who wanted to bring me in to mediate a case.

The client was a Jewish woman who was having a conflict with someone in their community. The woman struck the intake specialists as having "emotional issues" because she was speaking in an "agitated" manner, going on tangents, and expressing beliefs that the intake specialists felt were "paranoid." Moreover, she had mentioned she had a history of mental health problems. One particular fear that this woman had, was that someone in her Jewish community would discover she was at mediation, and for these reasons she requested a non-Jewish mediator to handle the case.

When I spoke to the case manager, they asked me if I would take the case because of the mental health issues involved. I followed the protocols we have been introducing in this book and asked why the case manager believed she needed special help, and, more importantly, if this woman had requested that help. It became clear that there were a lot of assumptions that help was needed, but the woman had not asked for it. Moreover, the entire team seemed uncomfortable as to how they could handle the potential challenging behaviors they were envisioning because they knew the woman had a mental health history. Linking mental health problems to problematic behaviors is a common mistake, which we will explore in chapter 6. (In chapter 9, we will also share tools to properly address behaviors without linking them to mental health problems.)

The most surprising aspect of this situation was that the case managers had asked for me, as I am culturally Jewish, and I have a Jewish-sounding last name—Berstein. The case manager said

---

44 Equal Employment Opportunity Commission (2002). *The ADA: A Primer for Small Business.* Retrieved from https://www.eeoc.gov/laws/guidance/ada-primer-small-business.

they had thought of a plan to address that: they wanted me to take the case without ever saying my last name, so that way the client would not realize I was Jewish. My initial response was to joke that I look ethnically Jewish, and I was surprised they believed we could really fool her in this manner. But my next point was that this team had done the opposite of what this woman had asked. Just because she mentioned a mental health history, they had sought to bring in extra mental health help even though the client never asked for it.

The one thing she had asked for was a chance to have a non-Jewish mediator—and they were doing the opposite. Moreover, they were acting like it was bizarre that she was paranoid without realizing she was right to be afraid—her impartial mediators were actively looking to sneak in a Jewish person as a mediator, against her wishes to protect her anonymity.

I explained all of this to the case managers, declined the case, and sent some training materials to help them with future cases. I share this story now to stress how misdirected we can become when we make assumptions based on someone's mental health disclosure. This team was well intentioned. They just were overwhelmed by their own assumptions and worried once they heard that there was a mental health history and once they perceived behaviors that they felt nervous about. The best practice here is to develop better tools for addressing challenging behaviors from all parties, as we will explore in chapter 9.

ii. Workplace Case Study: Responding to Disclosures at Work

Managers frequently offer informal disability accommodations to employees who reveal they have mental health needs, but then they run into problems. It is therefore important to follow a consistent process when responding to any potentially medical request. Take this scenario:

An employee approaches a manager and explains they cannot work because they are depressed over their partner's sudden death. The manager says that this is completely understandable and adds, "Take all of the time you need."

The employee takes some days off. Then, upon return to work, they begin a pattern of challenging workplace behaviors, including missed deadlines, low-quality work, requests for preferential choices of assignments, and irritable clashes with coworkers.

This pattern continues month after month, with the manager wondering about whether to confront the employee, and what to say because it appears that this employee may still be struggling to cope with the loss of their partner.

Finally, the manager decides enough is enough: other employees are complaining that it is unfair that the employee is receiving all of this special treatment. The manager decides to talk to the employee about their conduct and tells the employee, "I cut you slack, but now you have to get back to normal with your work." The employee replies, "What are you talking about? I thought this was a disability accommodation for my depression."

The ADA requires that most workplaces work with employees to offer job adjustments so that the employee can still perform the essential functions of their job despite the challenges presented by their disability. This is called a reasonable accommodation, and there is no simple one-size-fits-all procedure for asking for one or for assessing whether it is feasible. Instead, it happens on a case-by-case basis, which means that there is a lot of potential for possible mistakes and liability.

Any request for a change at work that is linked to a medical condition could potentially be a reasonable accommodation request.[45] Employees do not have to use the word "disability" or "reasonable accommodation," and they don't have to put their request in writing or suggest a solution to their problem. All they must do to trigger this obligation is to identify with a medical need and ask for a change because of it.

In our scenario of the employee who lost their partner, was their request a medical request? Because depression is a clinical condition that could be a source of disability, is it possible that it was a medical request? This manager may have made a mistake by not recognizing, from this colloquial-sounding language about a mental health need, that it could have been a disability request citing an actual clinical diagnosis. In other words, this manager may not have even realized this was a mental health disclosure at all. This case illustrates one problem that arises when there is an informal response to accommodating a health-related change at work. Now the manager may have liability for not responding to this disclosure as the manager would have regarding any other health disclosure.

For all of these reasons, it is best to use care in responding to health disclosures that are coupled with a request for a change at work. Any potential request for a reasonable accommodation, should be referred to human resources or whoever would be in charge of responding to such a request in your organization. If, however, the person discloses a possible mental health situation without asking for any change, then it is important not to make the paternalistic assumption they are asking you for help.

TAKEAWAY

At work, any request for a change, coupled with a potential medical need, may be a request for a reasonable accommodation.

C. WHEN THERE ARE ACCUSATIONS

Perhaps the most difficult way mental health needs can come up in a conflict is when one person accuses another of having mental health problems. Unfortunately, as we will learn in later chapters, there are still societal stigmas that are often inappropriately attached to someone having a mental illness, and people often use slurs and attacks related to mental health in order to undermine someone else. Of course, that is not the only way an accusation may arise. For example, an accusation can also be made in the case of two people who are in a caring relationship, one of whom genuinely believes the other needs help, and that is what leads to their suggestion that the other person is experiencing a mental health problem.

When one person has made a mental health accusation about another, a third-party conflict resolver has a lot of dynamics to manage. They may want to:

---

[45] Equal Employment Opportunity Commission (2002). The ADA: A Primer for Small Business. Retrieved from https://www.eeoc.gov/laws/guidance/ada-primer-small-business.

- Offer reassurances that they are not judging anyone based on their mental health.

- Check in about whether the accused is comfortable after being singled out and possibly stigmatized—all while not using a tone that adds stigma to the mental health accusation.

- Be available to act supportively if the accused decides to turn this into a disclosure and be ready to empower them through this process even though it was not their choice.

- Be ready to ignore any suspicions that the accusation engendered in our own minds.

- Find a way to respond to the accuser's feelings regarding the behavioral issues they linked to the accusation.

All of these issues are incredibly delicate to manage. There is no way to fake the various sensitivities involved, so it is important that you use the insights and tools like those presented in this book to develop an authentic empowerment mindset for when these topics come up. There is no simple answer.

Here is one possible starting point for what an effective introductory statement might look like when one is responding to an accusation from a hypothetical "Accuser":

Whenever mental health needs are discussed in a conflict, I always make sure to remind everyone that I am trying my best to be impartial and empowering surrounding mental health. I have received training to do this, I practice doing this, and whenever any accusations come up, I always respond in this same manner.

Anyone is welcome to disclose their mental health needs at any time during this conflict and if they want any changes because of them, I will work with them to do that. However, no one should ever be stigmatized for having mental health needs, or feel pressured to disclose them if they choose not to do so.

In this case, because Accuser is the one to raise it, I am going to treat it like it never came up at all and I will remind everyone it is not my role to make assessments about anyone's mental health anyway.

Please refrain from any more of these accusations, and instead let's just focus on the behaviors everyone is experiencing and discuss any feelings about those. In this case, Accuser seemed upset about Behavior so let's move on to discussing that behavior.

Of course, if anyone wants to discuss their mental health needs at any time, they are always welcome to do so, as if this accusation never happened. But that's their choice, nobody else's.

Now let's shift our attention back to Behavior.

This statement makes sure everyone understands that the conflict resolver has a general standard set of practices about mental health and is not singling out the accuser or the accused based on the accusation. It sets a tone of empowerment for anyone who has mental health needs, laying out some options for them but being sure to emphasize that the accusation bears no weight and that the conflict resolver does not really have any role in assessing someone's mental health. While reminding everyone involved how they can disclose mental health needs if they would like to, this statement removes any pressure to do so and does not ask that anyone do so. Instead, it models a shift away from mental health accusations and toward the behaviors they were related to: moving the conflict discussion forward to something that is appropriate to discuss, while hopefully deflating and deescalating the accusation.

TAKEAWAY

Accusations are very challenging. One approach is to use them as a reminder to share broad mental health practices and to model a shift away from mental health accusations toward the underlying behaviors that led to them.

D. WHEN WE SUSPECT

Human beings are natural guessers. Our brains, operating on instinct, are guessing all the time. Everything we see is filtered through our best supposition of what it means, and that includes our interpretations of any people or behaviors we encounter. There is no way to stop your brain from engaging in this activity, and so it is impossible for people not to form suspicions about someone's mental health situation from time to time.

Everyone occasionally suspects that other people have mental health problems. In forming these suspicions, they may have been influenced by any of the following:

- Amateur psychology knowledge from reading online personality quizzes, blogposts, articles, or anything else that discusses human behavior
- Personal experiences living with mental instability, supporting a loved one with mental instability, or being upset because of someone's mental instability
- Portrayals of mental instability in the news, literature, television, movies, podcasts, or any other media
- Some mental health education in school
- Professional training about mental health
- Introductory training about mental health that teaches techniques for recognizing mental health problems and that offer support, such as MHFA or comparable training
- Anything else from their life that gave them some ideas about mental health

In other words, mental health concepts are ubiquitous in our society and easily influence our perspectives. This is especially true for anyone who has been taught how to make a diagnosis or label a mental health problem in any way. If your brain has been exposed to this information, you will eventually start making inappropriate guesses about peoples' mental health.

While training is available to help you recognize and mitigate the unconscious biases that fuel these improper guesses, these implicit bias trainings have been shown to be flawed, often raising awareness without providing effective strategies to stop the biases.[46] That is why this book focuses on presenting concrete strategies in Part III that will prevent your biases from infiltrating the process, rather than assuming you will be able to remove them.

Instead of being mad at yourself for having bias, start thinking about developing a process that will ensure that your suspicions are less likely to lead you to take inappropriate actions. This entire book is designed to teach you procedurally fair techniques that will help you avoid problems.

We will develop procedurally fair processes in more depth during Part III. For now, note that the key way to manage suspicions is to divorce them from your decisions. To do that, first it is important to recognize that your thinking is biased. Next, remind yourself of your role in the conflict. Rather than assessing, labeling, and solving someone's mental health problem, your role is to help them feel heard and empowered. That way, they can feel free to make their own choices and they can work together with others in conflict to negotiate decisions that may be agreeable to all parties. By staying mindful of your role, you can remind yourself that your suspicions have no basis for being part of the conflict resolution process. Instead, you can complete the final step: strive to offer this person the same impartial treatment that you would provide to anyone, in a consistent manner that is not linked to your ideas about their mental health.

TAKEAWAY

It is natural to have biases and to form guesses about someone's mental health, but it is vital to divorce those guesses from your decisions about how to manage conflicts. Follow a consistent process that does not single anyone out for different treatment based on suspected mental health problems, and you will reduce the chance that you inadvertently discriminate based on your decisions.

i. Workplace Case Study: Library Disruptions

One day I received a call from a library foundation that was seeking mental illness sensitivity training for the libraries they managed. They explained that they had a problem with homeless patrons who would loiter in their libraries and disrupt two different kinds of events. Sometimes it would be an author speaking about a book, and these people would not stop interrupting. Other times, these people would interfere with classes being held at the libraries. They explained that their staff was not equipped to deal with people who had mental illnesses. For that reason, they were hoping I could provide them outside training to help them. Would I be able to offer them mental health sensitivity training?

I asked them if anyone had ever disclosed they had a mental illness, and they said no. For that matter, I also asked if anyone had disclosed being homeless, and again they said no. I then explained that, while mental health sensitivity training might help educate their staff and teach them ways to manage

---

[46] Hagiwara, N., Kron, F. W., Scerbo, M. W., & Watson, G. S. (2020). A call for grounding implicit bias training in clinical and translational frameworks. *Lancet, 395*(10234), 1457.

their suspicions, it would ultimately just help them learn to stop assuming these patrons have mental illnesses and instead focus on the behaviors at hand. But the mental health sensitivity training would not solve their problem. They had to address the reality that their staff was not prepared to deal with someone who disrupts their events, regardless of whether they have a mental health problem.

I explained that their deeper need was to make plans to deal with challenging behaviors so that their staff was ready to handle future disruptions. That is a separate training that has nothing to do with mental health because these challenging behaviors should never be correlated to mental health problems. Instead, we must break that link in everyone's minds and devise a protocol that will address the challenging event behaviors. We could do this through separate training regardless of whether anyone learns mental health sensitivity, and their staff would be prepared to handle those event problems.

This kind of confusion about the required training is very common. People interpret difficulties through the suspicions they form about mental health and lose sight of managing the disruptive behavior, which should not be presumed to be due to a mental health problem. All of the mental health etiquette training in the world is not going to help anyone know when to speak up when an author is being interrupted at the latest event. We will cover that kind of challenging behavior planning in chapter 9.

TAKEAWAY

Suspecting a mental health problem can lead you to act inappropriately. These suspicions can also stop you from addressing the real challenges you are facing. Avoid making these assumptions. Stay focused on your role, the process, and the behaviors you are observing.

ii. Family Case Study: Relapse Concerns

One common conflict in families arises when a family member is having a mental health relapse of some kind or they need to make adjustments to their treatment plan or even their diagnosis.

This is a case in which someone has a mental health problem and it is disclosed to their family, so although people know about it, now there are debates about it. In other words, there may be no dispute about whether or not a mental health problem generally exists, but the family members may have suspicions that there is some new instance of mental instability brewing. That means that they are still forming suspicions about mental health needs, and they are just arguing about whether there is a flare-up, even though the family may already agree about the diagnosis.

To be clear, families may not be wrong when they form these suspicions. Families have historically been seen both as aggravating mental health problems and supporting people through them, and mental health professionals have seen them as a potential burden as well as a resource.[47] In many cases, a

---

[47] Moen, Ø. L., Skundberg-Kletthagen, H., Lundquist, L. O., Gonzalez, M. T., & Schröder, A. (2020). The relationships between health professionals' perceived quality of care, family involvement and sense of coherence in community mental health services. *Issues in Mental Health Nursing*, 1–10.

family member may be seeing real signs of mental instability, such as the messiness or smoking seen as possible signs in earlier case studies.

The person living with the mental health problem may also be aware of this instability. It takes time to find a balance for their own definition of recovery, and their ideas about what they want may change over time. For example, one clinician who was trying to convince me to take more medication told me a story about a patient of his who took less medication during the times she wanted to write her plays, because she felt she was more creative when she was less medicated. Life is complicated. People have all sorts of decisions to make across the eight dimensions of wellness we explored in chapter 1, and they have every right to make whatever choices they want.

Families have often experienced their own traumas and worries that lead them to become more aggressive in pushing some kind of diagnosis or treatment plan. Often this ends up with their pushing their loved one further away. Someone who would have possibly sought their support in understanding the signs of a problem and navigating mental instability might end up feeling they have no other choice than to not discuss these things with their family at all. Sadly, this happens very often because people make the mistake of acting on their suspicions and assumptions instead of focusing on the empowerment techniques we detail in this book.

TAKEAWAY

Suspicions can be about more than whether a diagnosis exists; they could also be about whether there is some instability now. Acting on these suspicions can lead to communication breakdowns, strained relationships, and estrangements. It is best to stay focused on peoples' choices and behaviors rather than get stuck in our assumptions.

E. MENTAL HEALTH CONCERNS SCENARIOS

The scenarios presented in this section represent possible conflicts you may encounter, along with questions you can ask yourself to prepare how you might respond:

An employee is having frequent conflicts with another employee who they believe is experiencing mental health problems.

- What questions would you ask this employee to try to understand their conflict?
- How would you approach the other employee, if at all?

You have heard a rumor that your cousin has been diagnosed with a mental disorder.

- What will you do differently when you see them next?
- What do you think is okay to talk about? What is off limits?

Today has been a stressful day, and now you are in the grocery store. Someone is acting very bizarrely toward you. They are angry that you took the last cantaloupe, and they are following you around asking you if you would please give it to them. You don't think they seem well.

- What are you going to do about this situation?
- What assumptions do you make in this situation? How are they influencing you?

A friend of yours tells you they suffered from anxiety when they were younger and that it was severe. They had intensive therapy and were diagnosed with obsessive compulsive disorder. They say they are glad they got over that.

- What will you say in response to your friend?
- Does this new information make you see them differently? If so, how?

PART II

Dispelling Myths about Mental Illness

So far we have introduced mental health and mental illness, and we have begun exploring how these topics come up in the conflicts we see among family members, coworkers, and professional conflict resolvers.

We have also started to recognize some of the many challenges that are born out of the confusion surrounding mental health problems, as well as the assumptions we end up making as we try our best to avoid problems or support people who may be in need.

In all of these scenarios, we are fighting the current of myths that have led our entire society to develop fears and worries about mental health problems. These myths are corrosive to the empowerment we strive for when we are navigating conflicts. They are dangerous. And, worst of all, they are everywhere.

Even though I have spent over a decade working to reduce the power of these myths in the minds of others, I still have to wrestle with them every day in my own mind. We are all human, after all. Our minds are filled with biases and internalized stigmas.

Part II is about understanding why people have mental health concerns and appreciating the assumptions, paternalism, stigma, and scapegoating we all fall victim to from time to time. Then we dive into a few of the more pernicious myths, including the idea that we must label people as different from us in order to get them help; the notion that people with mental health problems must need special help; and the misunderstanding that mental health concerns have their own special link to challenging behaviors.

CHAPTER 3

WHY ARE PEOPLE CONCERNED?

As we explore the assumptions, paternalism, stigma, and scapegoating that occur, it is important to start with the premise that we are all human beings who share in these biased reactions from time to time (myself included).

I form assumptions about people, feel paternalistic impulses to intervene in someone else's life, harbor stigmatizing attitudes, and end up scapegoating mental health dynamics for problems caused by other issues. While these are destructive impulses, and we should all endeavor to correct them within ourselves, they are still understandably human responses to complicated situations. My intent is not to criticize you if your mind wanders toward these kinds of thoughts. Rather, the techniques we explore are tools that provide some step-by-step processes to act in impartial ways despite the inevitable fallibility we all share as human beings.

I call impartiality an aspirational goal because no person can ever be totally free of their unconscious bias and imperfect decision making. The goal here is to recognize the need to do better and to keep trying to do our best without being too hard on ourselves when we catch ourselves having a biased attitude. That kind of defensiveness makes it hard to be in a position to recognize these problems and improve. Therefore, as we work through these concerns, let us approach each of these issues with self-compassion and compassion for anyone who may find themselves manifesting any of these challenges.

TAKEAWAY

We're only human. Instead of beating ourselves up for our biases and mistakes, practice self-compassion and keep an open mind for opportunities for growth. We will never be perfectly impartial, but we can develop fairer processes in conflicts by following the principles in this book.

A. ASSUMPTIONS

We have already been exploring and questioning assumptions throughout this book. We make assumptions when we offer our own guesses or inferences. In simple terms, we make assumptions when we automatically fill in the blanks, and typically these ideas occur unconsciously. Our brain fills in the blank spaces without realizing that there were blank spaces there to begin with.

Why do we make these kinds of assumptions? It is human nature. Our brain is a sense-making organ that literally constructs pictures of reality for us.[48] It fills in gaps in the pictures our eyes take every moment, showing us the world. It adds layers of meaning on top of it to make sense of it. And it uses all sorts of heuristics and algorithms to try to keep us safe and prepared for any possible risks.

Unfortunately, that means we may automatically make all sorts of different assumptions about a person based on their gender, sexual orientation, race, disability, and so forth. Those kinds of assumptions can become especially dangerous when mental health problems are involved.

Although there are some cultural differences in how different social groups respond to mental health problems, and some practitioner biases in how different conditions get pathologized in the first place, mental health is still considered to be somewhat of a great equalizer. Mental illness occurs across all different races, sexual orientations, and social classes. Because of this universality across demographics, people often think it is okay to generalize. Yet, those generalizations are often based on a lot of missing information because most people are careful about disclosing their mental health problems.[49] Our society is left with skewed media portrayals.

Thus, when people hear I have bipolar disorder, they often assume that I'm in need of help, unreliable, or even dangerous. These are some of the many assumptions that we all have paved throughout the highways of our brains. They are some of the roads that lead us to form concerns when someone has a mental illness.

It is our responsibility to manage those concerns appropriately. This book is guiding you to a mindset to do exactly that, while also providing the tools that will help you develop your own process for counteracting these assumptions through effective mental health communication, impartial responses to challenging behaviors, and universally accessible processes that allow us to respond to anyone's needs regardless of whether they have a mental health condition.

TAKEAWAY

Keep an open mind, challenge your assumptions, and avoid trusting your gut. Instead, follow universal, impartial processes for talking about mental health, addressing challenging behaviors, and being accessible to people's needs.

i. Family Case Study: "You're Not Taking Your Medication"

For this case study, we are revisiting the couple whose daughter came home from college and started smoking in the house, and we will go deeper into understanding the assumptions present in that situation.

---

[48] Eagleman, David. (2011). *Incognito (Enhanced Edition): The secret lives of the brain.* Knopf.

[49] Reavley, N. J., Morgan, A. J., & Jorm, A. F. (2018). Disclosure of mental health problems: Findings from an Australian national survey. *Epidemiology and Psychiatric Sciences, 27*(4), 346–356.

As a refresher, this couple shared that they were upset that their daughter seemed to be sick with a mental health problem again. They said that normally she understands and follows all the rules of the house, and things are comfortable for everyone. One of these rules is that you cannot smoke in the home—you must smoke outside. Now, their daughter was smoking in the house. They said, "I know this means she is sick. She never does this unless she is sick and so I told her she needs to take her medication."

Did you notice the assumptions that were made here? This couple assumed that the only reason their daughter would not follow the house rules, or at least this no smoking rule, was that she was suffering symptoms from her mental disorder. That was the first assumption. The second assumption was that if she is suffering symptoms from her mental disorder, it must mean she was not taking her medication.

Both of these assumptions are flawed and destructive to the conflict resolution process. Yes, it could be true that their daughter was not able to keep up with the house rules because of her mental health condition. If that is the case, however, it is up to her to decide that for herself. Interpreting every behavior immediately through the lens of mental illness can be dehumanizing and offensive, and it can put a person on the defensive. Once the situation has been inflamed by these guesses, it might be difficult to collaboratively address the behavior problem and brainstorm ways to address it—one of which might be seeking mental health support.

Imagine the nonproductive fights that could be triggered and distract from the discussion of the actual behavior:

- Why do you make everything about my mental illness?

- You don't even see me as a person anymore; all you see is my disorder!

- There is no point sharing anything with you if all you are going to do is use it as evidence that you think I'm sick!

- Nothing will ever be the same as it was because this is what you always do now. . . .

These are just some examples of the endless cascade of conflicts that can arise when one acts on assumptions that someone might be experiencing illness symptoms. Moreover, that list of conflicts doesn't include the fights about whether there is a condition at all, whether to trust the doctor(s), how to interpret what the doctor(s) said, what is the best treatment plan, and whether we believe the person is following the treatment plan. Many fights could be avoided by shifting the conversation to a discussion of the behavior.

Instead of saying "I think you are sick," this family would be better off having an open conversation with their daughter about why she is smoking inside the house. It may be that the behavior is not related to illness at all, or that their daughter may express that she is struggling and wants support. Whatever is really going on, the focus on the behavior ensures that our assumptions are not controlling the conflict. It allows everyone to work out solutions together, even if they are still living amidst a backdrop of ongoing mental health concerns and debates about care.

The second assumption made here was that, if their daughter was sick, she must be off her medication. That is a flawed assumption. Medication is challenging and it does not always work. Someone can be taking the medication that may never actually work. Or it may work for a time and stop working, it may work but lead to side effects, or it may be affected by a drug interaction. It's also possible that the person may experience new trauma and stress so that the medication is no longer enough. Someone also has the right to pursue alternative treatment options, or no treatment at all, if that is what they choose. Medication is complicated.

There is an inaccurate notion that mental health problems are easily solved if the person would only take a certain medication. That is not the reality for everyone, and we should never assume it is the case in conflicts. If we drop these assumptions and instead focus on open-minded, open-ended interactions, we may be better able to resolve the conflict.

TAKEAWAY

To facilitate productive family conflict resolution, it may be best to focus on the behaviors and stop yourself from letting your assumptions guide you into a host of tangential, intractable conflicts.

ii. Workplace Case Study: Assuming Someone Needs Help

Workplaces have different cultures when it comes to mental health. Some believe in health promotion. Accordingly, they may send out announcements about recreational activities, yoga, meditation, and other well-being-related benefits. They may also try to promote mental health support on a regular basis. This is often done through the use of an outside vendor known as an employee assistance plan, or EAP, which includes benefits related to emotional well-being such as short-term counseling and other services.

Other workplaces may have processes like these EAPs in place, but it is still seen as undesirable for people to access that kind of help or take time off for their well-being. These are often "workaholic" environments that prize longer hours, limited work-life balance, regular stress, and the like as a badge of honor that shows how serious everyone is about working. Of course, many companies fall somewhere in between these types.

Wherever a company falls on this spectrum, they often come to me with the same question: what is the best way to tell an employee who seems to have a mental health problem that they need to get help? In other words, how can I refer an employee to the EAP?

In one company focused on well-being, a manager said she had an employee who came to her office every day for hours of support. She did not know how to tell them that this was too much and that they needed help. She was afraid they would feel rejected or would be singled out because she had told all of her employees that her door was always open. How could she close it now? What should she do?

In another company that did not have an open-door policy, a manager told me she was concerned about an employee who was experiencing a lot of interpersonal conflicts and missing deadlines. But they never talked about anything outside of their work, and she was wondering how to approach this person and offer them a referral to the EAP?

Both of these managers are making the same assumption. That is, they are assuming that the behavior problem they are noticing requires help from the EAP.

Why are they uneasy about broaching the topic? They might be afraid to have a tricky conversation about the employee's mental health because that really is an inappropriate conversation, given that the employee has not decided to talk about it. These managers jumped to their assumption that the challenging behaviors they were seeing—the long talks, interpersonal conflicts, missed deadlines—were symptoms of mental health problems. Now they are struggling to have a mental health conversation they really should not be starting at all.

Whether or not your workplace is offering resources, and whether or not your workplace has an EAP, the manager's role is to discuss employee behavior with them—not diagnose or point out a mental health problem. Therefore, their conversations should focus solely on addressing the behavior.

Chapter 8 will cover ways to engage in mental health promotion through universal practices with behavior-based criteria that do not single anyone out. For now, note the problems that arise when we make the assumption that this person needs the EAP instead of talking about their behavior.

TAKEAWAY

In workplace settings, focus on your role and on the behaviors that affect the workplace instead of assuming that mental health is involved with the challenging behaviors you are seeing.

B. PATERNALISM

Paternalism is the idea that someone needs our help rather than trusting them to make their own choices. It is a disempowering concept when it affects anyone, but there are special wrinkles when mental health concerns are involved. That is because there are times when, legally, someone is not able to make their own decisions because they have been deemed incapable to do so on the grounds of impaired capacity due to their mental illness.

Broadly speaking, this happens in two major contexts. The first is involuntary commitment, when someone is compelled to go into treatment against their will on either an inpatient basis (what we normally think of when we think civil commitment, taken to a hospital) or on an outpatient basis (a newer model of commitment where someone has a legal order to receive compulsory treatment while not being kept on an inpatient basis).[50] When someone has been committed, they have had some autonomy taken away from them.

---

[50] Monahan, J., & Shah, S. A. (1989). Dangerousness and commitment of the mentally disordered in the United States. *Schizophrenia Bulletin, 15*(4), 541; Testa, M., & West, S. G. (2010). Civil commitment in the United States. *Psychiatry, 7*(10), 30.

The other context in which this happens is guardianship, when someone's decision-making power is transferred to someone else. This can happen when someone is an adult, or it is also the reality for children who have parents and legal guardians that control their mental health care.

During one training I gave to court judges, a judge asked what they should do for a case where the parents were divorced, and they had a split custody arrangement for a child who may have a mental health problem. When the child was in one parent's custody, that parent gave their medication, but the other parent did not believe it was a mental health problem and so they would not.

I suggested they go to a mediator to help the parents decide what they believe is best for the child. But nowhere in the question was there any sentiment about what the child wanted because, again, the decisions go to the guardian.

When someone has been committed or placed under guardianship, they are in an inherently paternalistic situation surrounding their mental health. In those cases, it may become necessary or appropriate for their decisions to be overridden, but you can still apply the techniques in this book to discuss the conflicts with them in an empowering manner.

We are discussing these situations now to help you understand that there are mechanisms designed to help people deemed unable to make their own choices if someone is really in need of that level of support. However, that is rare. If you are not at that point with your loved one, coworker, or anyone you are interacting with, then it is not appropriate for you to adopt a paternalistic posture toward them. Simply put, everyone is in charge of their own lives and choices unless they have been committed, have a guardian, or have been arrested or incarcerated. Even in any of these circumstances, while they technically may have lost some autonomy rights, they still deserve to be spoken to in an empowering manner.

It may seem extreme to invoke these limits of autonomy, but I have found this point essential in helping people accept that someone else's mental health problem is not something for us to fix. It is their personal situation, and they are entitled to make their own choices.

It is important for everyone to feel empowered about their lives and to know they have a voice in whatever conflicts they are experiencing.

TAKEAWAY

Unless your situation involves a commitment or guardianship dynamic, it is not appropriate to act paternalistically toward a person with a mental health problem. Even in those extreme situations where their choices are overridden, you can still use the techniques described in this book to treat them with respect and help them feel more empowered.

i. Personal Story: "What Did the Doctor Say?"

As is true of many families, mine showed great deference to the doctor's opinion about my mental illness rather than sharing their own perspectives. Yet, as we discussed earlier, the reality is that a mental health professional's opinion is generally not a definitive answer. Different professionals may disagree, and ultimately it is the client's choice of who to listen to and how they want to manage their care. In fact, many mental health professionals will recognize this as they build alignment with their clients. They will emphasize that they are not there to provide direction and that the sessions instead occur at the direction of the client. They will also acknowledge that they do not have any perfect or definitive answers and that they are using their best judgment to offer constructive advice.

This was my experience, more or less, with my first psychiatrist and most of my clinicians since. While my family would constantly ask me what the psychiatrist said to do, as if it was an answer they would follow, my psychiatrist would spend my session asking me what I wanted to do. He understood that his role was to foster my autonomy, and he cared about empowering me to make my own choices. Most clinicians will adopt this position because they have a professional responsibility to protect their client's rights and support them in making their own choices.

My parents did not understand this viewpoint, however. No matter what I said, they persisted in the thought that the psychiatrist had all of the answers and that we had to do whatever they said. This led me to adopt a pattern whereby I would tell my psychiatrist what I wanted to do, such as return to college the next semester instead of waiting a year or not take a part-time job during my semester in recovery. I would then ask him if he thought this sounded like a good idea, and he would always say yes. Then I would tell my parents the doctor said it was a good idea, and they would do whatever I wanted. For years, I would get my doctor's rubber-stamp approval for all of my important decisions and my parents would adhere to it as if it was the gospel.

I share this story to demonstrate the kinds of communication breakdowns that occur when paternalism becomes part of the equation. My parents and I lost the opportunity to discuss my various options because they stopped seeing that these were my choices to make. Instead, we were all left using my psychiatrist's seal of approval as the arbiter of all of my important life choices. I found a way to make that feel somewhat functional for me, thanks to the fact that my family did not understand how therapy actually works. But ultimately this was still a dysfunctional situation: I was disappointed by my family's deference to my doctor instead of their caring to hear my voice, and I was left without the family support I craved as I made my decisions.

Even when a person has a mental health clinician they rely on and trust, they still make choices about their treatment and their life. It is important to focus on hearing their voice and supporting their decision making rather than paternalistically deferring to treatment providers.

ii. Workplace Case Study: Concerns about Destructive Delusions

Many people have asked me what to do when they encounter a seemingly bizarre belief that they think may be a delusion and a sign of a mental health problem. Workplaces, families, and conflict resolvers all seek support in forming the best response to thoughts that do not seem rooted in reality.

My recommendation in these situations is to start by asking yourself what your role is. Are you in charge of auditing someone's beliefs, assessing their veracity, and intervening in some way? In most cases, the answer is no.

The next question is: What are you responsible for addressing? Usually, this line of inquiry leads to a different challenging behavior that is the real issue. We will discuss challenging behaviors in more depth in chapter 9.

A complaint about a delusion may actually be rooted in a challenging behavior, and I always discover that underlying behavior by asking the simple question, "Why is this belief a problem for you?" Most often it is a problem because the person feels uncomfortable repeatedly discussing this issue at length. In that case, it is really just an issue of monopolization of time, and the solution may be to remind the person of not going over a certain amount of time or frequency of contact. There is no need to attempt to correct the potential delusion.

Other times the problem is not the bizarre-seeming belief itself, but rather that it was communicated along with some kind of threat or offensive language, such as something racist. In those cases, the problem is not the beliefs but rather the threat or the offensive content.

We will discuss this process of decoupling challenging behaviors from mental health concerns later on in chapter 9. Right now, it is important to note that judging someone's beliefs as "off" is a common form of paternalism because it assumes we know better about what they should believe.

We may not agree with someone else's religious beliefs if they differ from our own, and we may privately feel their religion is a delusional belief system that is not at all true. Yet typically, we would not feel inclined to confront or correct another person's religious beliefs. Instead, we respect their choice to hold those beliefs without a confrontation. The same goes for whatever someone chooses to believe, unless you have a role in auditing their beliefs. Otherwise, it is important to assess if someone's behavior is a problem—not their beliefs.

TAKEAWAY

Judging someone's beliefs or behavior as possibly related to a mental health problem and deciding to treat a person differently based on that perception is a form of paternalism that is inappropriate. Instead of acting paternalistically, focus on your actual role and on addressing challenging behaviors that fit your role.

iii. Conflict Resolver Case Study: Behind-the-Scenes Changes

Some professional conflict resolvers believe it is important to assess their clients' personalities or mental health needs and to tailor their approach to their clients based on that assessment. Although this is a relatively common practice, it often violates the core values of impartiality and self-determination.

It is not fair because the conflict resolver is forming a bias based on their private assessment of the party's mental health situation, and they are letting that bias influence the conflict resolution process. This approach also violates self-determination because it is done without the client's knowledge or buy-in. In other words, the client did not come seeking the mental health profile, and therefore it was done against their will.

People who perform these kinds of behind-the-scenes profiling and process changes typically have good intentions. They want to provide the best service to their clients and to meet their needs. Unfortunately, their desire to do so leads them to forget that it is not their role to provide these services.

It is not appropriate for conflict resolvers to become paternalistic and offer a process they believe is especially good for a certain kind of mental health dynamic.

TAKEAWAY

Unless clients have asked you to do a mental health assessment and offer tailored services, and it fits your role to do so, do not do one. Any changes you make based on that assessment are a source of bias.

C. STIGMA

Stigma can be a confusing concept, and like many of the other terms we have discussed related to mental health, it is hard to define. Often it is something we know when we see it, yet it can also be very difficult to see.

Bernice Pescosolido is a sociologist who has researched the stigma surrounding mental illness extensively and has done important work explaining the core concepts underlying it. She explains that researchers define stigma as a mark, condition, or status that is being devalued, while stigmatization is the process where that mark affects the people touched by it—a process that happens through labeling differences, associating the differences with negative stereotypes, separating people into an "us" and a "them," and experiencing some kind of discrimination or loss of status.[51] People get labeled with mental health conditions, associated with stereotypes, separated out, and then otherwise diminished. Sadly, a few of the great many ways someone with a mental health condition may be wrongly stigmatized is by assuming they should feel shame about their condition; that they are inferior intellectually and otherwise incapable; that they are dangerous and should be feared; or that they are uncomfortable to have around and should be excluded.

Stigma can be pervasive and affect all kinds of mental health stakeholders. Pescosolido distinguishes between perceived stigma (the belief someone may devalue a person with a mental health condition), endorsed stigma (the expression of agreement with prejudices and stereotypes), anticipated stigma (the expectation of experiencing discrimination), received stigma (the experience of rejection, devaluation, and discrimination), and enacted stigma (the behaviors of stigmatizers providing differential treatment). Further, stigma has been divided into several different types based on where it lies, including: internalized stigma, which occurs when someone begins to adopt stigmatizing attitudes toward themselves; courtesy stigma, which gets applied to loved ones and others associated with a person with a mental health condition; public stigma, which becomes an attitude prevalent in the general population; provider-based stigma, which manifests in mental health service providers who develop prejudices about their clientele; and structural or institutional stigma, which ends up codified in policies, laws, and practices. Research shows that stigma is ubiquitous across countries and cultures. It affects most people living with mental health problems as they seek work or build relationships, and it is caused by a wide

---

[51] Pescosolido, B. A., & Martin, J. K. (2015). The stigma complex. *Annual Review of Sociology, 41*, 87–116.

variety of sources, including behaviors from micro-level individuals to macro-level influencers of mass media and society at large.[52]

Pescosolido has provided a helpful historical background of how stigma came to be discussed among sociologists. She writes that the sociology field began discussing stigma in earnest in the 1960s, often with a focus on how labels create stigma beyond any behaviors that are being critiqued. She also describes how research purporting that stigma decreased in the 1990s led to more attention to the topic.[53] Pescosolido concluded that the public had become more open to disclosure, recognition, and response regarding mental health problems but that stigma still persisted: there were still challenges in achieving social acceptance, increased rejection and social distance were still the case, and there was little power to change either. She noted that the stigmatizing associations between violence and mental illness constituted one example of the ongoing, pervasive problem. Although children tended to elicit more sympathy than adults, there was a noted negativity toward childhood depression, which was seen as very serious, unlikely to improve, and likely to be linked to violence.

Self-stigma is particularly dangerous. When people are aware of societal negative attitudes toward their condition, they start to agree with these stereotypes. They then might apply the stereotypes to themselves, thereby decreasing their sense of self-esteem and self-efficacy.[54] This internalized stigma is known to lead to poorer prognoses.[55,56] High levels of stigma are correlated with poor insight, low amounts of hope, poor self-esteem, poor social functioning, impaired quality of life, and less sense of the meaning in life.[57,58]

Understanding the pervasive impact of this stigma helps us appreciate how desperately people living with all kinds of mental health issues need to be empowered. It helps drive home the necessity that we work on the practices proposed in this book. In that way we can, hopefully, reduce the impact of our personal stereotypes and use conflict resolution best practices to decrease the amount of stigma affecting whoever we are in conflict with or whoever we are mediating between.

Bear in mind that this stigma is not just limited to diagnosable mental health problems. All kinds of feelings, emotions, and mental health activities may be stigmatized; thus, it is helpful for us to normalize the full spectrum of mental health when we approach the conflicts we encounter.

---

[52] Rössler, W. (2016). The stigma of mental disorders: A millennia-long history of social exclusion and prejudices. *EMBO Reports, 17*(9), 1250–1253.

[53] Pescosolido, B. A. (2013). The public stigma of mental illness: What do we think; what do we know; what can we prove?. *Journal of Health and Social Behavior, 54*(1), 1–21.

[54] Corrigan, P. W., & Rao, D. (2012). On the self-stigma of mental illness: Stages, disclosure, and strategies for change. *Canadian Journal of Psychiatry. Revue canadienne de psychiatrie, 57*(8), 464–469.

[55] Boyd, J. E., Adler, E. P., Otilingam, P. G., & Peters, T. (2014). Internalized Stigma of Mental Illness (ISMI) Scale: A multinational review. *Comprehensive Psychiatry, 55*(1), 221–231.

[56] NIMH. National Institute of Mental Health Strategic Plan. Washington DC: U.S. Department of Health & Human Services; 2008 [Report No.: NIH Publication No. 08–6368]

[57] Ehrlich-Ben Or, S., Hasson-Ohayon, I., Feingold, D., Vahab, K., Amiaz, R., Weiser, M., & Lysaker, P. H. (2013). Meaning in life, insight and self-stigma among people with severe mental illness. *Comprehensive Psychiatry, 54*(2), 195–200.

[58] Mashiach-Eizenberg, M., Hasson-Ohayon, I., Yanos, P. T., Lysaker, P. H., & Roe, D. (2013). Internalized stigma and quality of life among persons with severe mental illness: The mediating roles of self-esteem and hope. *Psychiatry Research, 208*(1), 15–20.

TAKEAWAY

Stigma includes the negative attitudes inappropriately associated with a mental health condition. These attitudes can be extremely destructive, including the source of discrimination and negative internalized beliefs. Sadly, they are pervasive throughout our society.

i. Personal Story: Blatant and Subtle Stigma

Stigma is all about attitudes. Traditionally, we tend to think about stigma in the most sensationalist fashion. A couple of years after my initial diagnosis, I was 21 and working as a research analyst in Philadelphia. I decided to tell someone I was seeing that I had bipolar disorder and that I did mental health advocacy work in addition to my job. She froze and told me that her cousin was molested by someone with bipolar disorder. She asked me to leave, and I never saw her again. That is one example of blatant stigma associated with a mental health diagnosis—the idea that anyone with a mental health label may be undesirable, and the stereotyping that emerges because of a sensational example that may have come from the media or, in this case, the woman's family history.

There are also many less obvious kinds of stigma, which manifest more subtly as microaggressions—and often with good intentions. When I was applying for graduate school and I told a mentor with whom I had a longstanding history that I had decided to go public with my mental illness, he was surprised to learn that I had bipolar disorder because I had never told him before. "That's fine," he said. "My stepson also has bipolar disorder, and it's fine as long as you take your Lithium."

This was a wonderful, caring man who was completely well intentioned, but he was perpetuating multiple stigmatizing attitudes. First, he was removing my choice by presuming there was one right way to handle this condition—Lithium. Second, he was implying that if someone experiences instability, it is because they are mistakenly not taking this medication.

What about support groups? When I was involved in mood disorder support groups, the topic of when to tell a romantic partner about a mental health condition would often come up. Many people talked about the challenges they had keeping their condition secret, hiding their medications when someone slept over, and fearing the person might leave them if they did not get to know them before fielding the "bad news" about their living with a mental health problem. This well-meaning advice, too, amplified the sense of stigma surrounding mental health conditions. There were many ways that we shared tips to cope with the stigma that inadvertently expanded its scope.

Problems also occur among advocacy groups. I first started speaking about my mental illness through a speaker's bureau associated with a mental health advocacy group. The advocacy group had a policy that a person who had mental health problems could not be a speaker unless they had been out of the hospital for at least 9 months. But when I met the group, I was only 4 months out of the hospital. I therefore assumed that I would have to wait to be a speaker. Then the director saw me. To my surprise, she became very excited and said she would waive the policy for me because I seemed more articulate than she had expected and because of how I looked (she explained that she had found it hard to find speakers who were not overweight due to medication side effects). On first blush, this might seem a positive experience to be complimented, but it was painful to be seen in this manner and to hear the stereotypes from this advocacy organization.

ii. The Dangers of Profiling Some Parties as "High Conflict"

In recent years, there has been a rise in trainings that advise conflict resolvers to screen for challenging clients and then treat those parties differently based on unshared labels. These models explicitly or indirectly encourage mediators to profile their clients based on different personality types, neurodevelopmental experiences, or violence risk factors. Some of these trainings teach mediators to adapt their practices to "high-conflict personalities," to "recognize neurodevelopmental differences," or to think about which anatomical parts of the brain might be driving client actions.

These models often heap stigma on the labeled parties, which is clear simply by reviewing the marketing tactics describing how terrible it is to work with a "difficult person." Although it is not discriminatory under the ADA to describe someone as a "difficult person," sometimes proxy labels related to personality can be seen as ways someone might end up discriminating against parties on the basis of mental disorders.

These labels were likely not created with ill intentions. At first glance, it may seem that this kind of segmentation can empower mediators to better serve the needs of their clients and better protect their safety. But this label-focused solution is misguided. It is actually disempowering to parties, it can diminish the quality of mediation sessions, and it could potentially create a heightened risk of liability under the ADA, which considers it illegal to treat someone differently based on the presence or suspicion of having a disability.

This book is not designed to teach you to assess the chances that you may be held liable for a specific potential act of discrimination, particularly given that I do not agree with some of the unfortunate stigmatizing disparities that can make it harder to make psychiatric claims under the ADA. However, to discourage profiling, I will demonstrate how engaging in labeling could potentially open someone up to liability under the ADA. This becomes a stronger possibility as enforcement of the law evolves along with our social norms and as people become more assertive in asking for accommodations at work and in making discrimination claims.[59]

As mentioned in the "Appreciating Discrimination" section at the start of this book, enforcement of discrimination claims under the ADA and other laws can be challenging and disparately harder for someone making such a claim based on a mental health condition.[60] Moreover, liability for mediators

---

[59] Von Schrader, S., Malzer, V., & Bruyère, S. (2014). Perspectives on disability disclosure: The importance of employer practices and workplace climate. *Employee Responsibilities and Rights Journal, 26*(4), 237–255; Nevala, N., Pehkonen, I., Koskela, I., Ruusuvuori, J., & Anttila, H. (2015). Workplace accommodation among persons with disabilities: A systematic review of its effectiveness and barriers or facilitators. *Journal of Occupational Rehabilitation, 25*(2), 432–448; Hickox, S. A., & Hall, A. (2018). Atypical accommodations for employees with psychiatric disabilities. *American Business Law Journal, 55*(3), 537–594.

[60] Kaminer, D. N. (2016). Mentally ill employees in the workplace: Does the ADA Amendments Act provide adequate protection. *Health Matrix, 26*, 205; Swanson, J., Burris, S., Moss, K., & Ullman, M. (2006); Stefan, S. (2000). Delusions of Rights: Americans with Psychiatric Disabilities, Employment Discrimination and the Americans with Disabilities Act. *Alabama Law Review, 52*, 271.

and other dispute resolvers can be rare as well due to a variety of factors, perhaps first and foremost because parties are unaware of their rights and appropriate expectations and thus are less likely to hold their mediator accountable.[61] Historically, issues of personality and temperament have generally been distinguished from other mental disorders. Moreover, it has often been hard for plaintiffs to make a prima facie case that discrimination has occurred based on their testimony that an employer, for instance, has treated them differently based on their perceived personality deficits.[62]

It has been similarly difficult for those with a psychiatric condition to provide enough evidence that their employer regarded them as so disabled by their mental health condition that they would be, more broadly, substantially limited from a major life activity and thus considered to be truly disabled under the ADA.[63] For instance, when a county knew of a deputy's posttraumatic stress disorder (PTSD) diagnosis, gave the deputy a psychological examination, and took steps to accommodate the PTSD, one court held this was not enough to show the county regarded that person as disabled by their PTSD for the purposes of a discrimination claim.[64]

Enforcement has evolved with amendments and can vary in different jurisdictions. Generally, however, a major question arises when it comes to discrimination: Does the offending party believe the person to be disabled, being substantially limited in a major life activity?[65] Is there evidence to prove this disability?

When "high-conflict personalities" are considered to likely be a product of a personality disorder and a practitioner treats people with this label as if they are substantially limited and unable to improve, then this can become evidence that the practitioner did regard that party as having a disability. If this logic is manifested by the trainings in which a practitioner participated, or in their policies, practices, and comments, then this could potentially show a court that they were seen as having a disability. In other words, the use of this profiling framework to identify "high-conflict people" who are seen as not being able to change may create the proof needed to show the different treatment was based on the perception that the party had a disability.

Again, every claim is evaluated on a case-by-case basis. One case with an e-mail record that said "to diagnose insanity would mean to find there is a brain" did not, in a court's eyes, amount to the person being regarded as disabled based on their depression. The reason was that the court distinguished perceived intelligence from ability to think.[66] In another case, a social worker was able to sufficiently state

---

[61] Bultena, C., Ramser, C., & Tilker, K. (2019). Mediation madness V: Misfit mediators. *Southern Journal of Business and Ethics, 11*, 53–75.

[62] Smith, D. M. (2006). The paradox of personality: Mental illness, employment discrimination, and the Americans with Disabilities Act. *George Mason University Civil Rights Law Journal, 17*, 79; Gonzalez, M. F., Capman, J. F., Martin, N. R., Johnson, T. M., Theys, E. R., & Boyce, A. S. (2019). Personality and the ADA: Ameliorating fairness concerns and maintaining utility. *Industrial and Organizational Psychology, 12*(2), 151–156.

[63] Justice disparities: Does the ADA enforcement system treat people with psychiatric disabilities fairly? *Maryland Law Review, 66*, 94.

[64] Magdaleno v. Washington County, 277 Fed. Appx. 679 (9th Cir. 2008).

[65] Concannon, J. (2012). Mind matters: Mental disability and the history and future of the Americans with Disabilities Act. *Law and Psychological Review, 36*, 89; Randolph, J. N. (2006). Problem employees: Merely cantankerous or substantially limited in their ability to interact with others? *University of Cincinnati Law Review, 74*(3), 1135–1156.

[66] Furry v. Lehigh Valley Health System, 902 F. Supp. 2d 645 (E.D. Pa. 2012).

her employer regarded her as disabled in part because the supervisor had represented to others their belief that she was not able to make sound decisions because of her anxiety, including accusations that she had been harassing coworkers with after-hours calls due to her anxiety, which her supervisor believed caused her to develop an irrational desire to close out cases.[67]

Implementation of the law is often nebulous. It can be difficult to pursue psychiatric ADA discrimination claims, especially given the absence of clear evidence that someone is truly being treated differently based on their disability or they are truly seen as unable to function because of that disability. It can be particularly difficult to recover for claims of discrimination related to personality disorders, which are often treated with more stigma than other psychiatric conditions. Yet when there are training materials that deliberately suggest treating people differently based on the premise that parties are debilitated by personality disorders, these practices may provide a fact pattern that could sway a court. These programs could potentially serve as evidence that prejudice toward a party was indeed due to a broader belief that the party was limited by their personality-related disability as opposed to the peccadillos of their specific personality presentation that manifested that day.

Moreover, this analysis is about how a court may review a potential disability discrimination claim under the law. There are other steps that may be taken before legal action commences, including informal allegations. While people with claims based on mental disorders may be less likely to make such claims due to their desire not to disclose and to avoid stigma, or due to other difficulties they may experience in making a case, people with mental health disorders are not precluded from speaking up. More and more, people are comfortable being open about their conditions and they are learning to self-advocate through non-legal mechanisms such as grievances at organizations, or through public advocacy. It therefore may be less fraught if practitioners and trainers stop the labeling and just focus on teaching behavior-focused, challenging behavior programs, similar to the material we will cover in chapter 9.

TAKEAWAY

Although it can be difficult for someone with a mental health disability to complain due to stigma and the challenges demonstrating discrimination, labeling people can still provide evidence supporting a discrimination claim.

iii. Conflict Resolver Case Study: Published Guidelines and Inadvertent Stigma

Another well-meaning, inadvertently stigmatizing conflict resolver protocol was the Association for Conflict Resolution's (ACR's) Guidelines for Safety Planning in Alternative Dispute Resolution (ADR), which suggested special protocols for "potentially violent individuals."[68] These screening protocols were released in 2014, and they were explicitly said to be based on a book written by a crisis intervention trainer and hostage negotiator, as well as on a personal conversation between a mediator and a second

---

[67] Ingram v. District of Columbia Child and Family Services Agency, 394 F. Supp. 3d 119 (D.D.C. 2019).

[68] This guidance was available at https://acrnet.org/page/ADR but has since been taken down to be updated.

former crisis negotiator. Using these sources, they advised that all dispute resolution practitioners see folks differently based on some sensitive identity categories, including some mental health experiences and disabilities. The guidelines were posted by a variety of groups including the ACR, the National Association for Community Mediation, and others.

One thing the ACR Guidelines do well is create general safety protocols and suggest that mediators think about having a universal process in place to address safety concerns similar to the techniques we will-outline for challenging behaviors in chapter 9. However, their protocols also included a guideline for presenting a special protocol for "potentially violent individuals" (Section A.1.e.).

Who was potentially violent according to the ACR Guidelines? Section B.2's list of assessment factors suggested that mediators be wary of "abuse victims" (Section B.2.e), victims with head trauma or PTSD (Section B.2.f), those who have recently experienced a loss (Section B.2.i), those experiencing chronic pain or illness (Section B.2.1), and people exhibiting psychological symptoms (Section B.2.n). All of these people were to be seen as potential threats and treated differently under Section A.1.e. In other words, this list added some stigma onto all of these labels.

But there is another way to address violent behaviors that does not profile people based on their history of abuse, victimization, or psychological adversity. Instead of asking mediators to be wary of these vulnerable populations, we can be equally vigilant and respectful with every party. Issue the same safety protocol, and adapt it based on observed behaviors rather than stereotypes based on the parties' history of PTSD or abuse. The ACR Guidelines offered a promising start by providing mediators with a detailed checklist for creating universal safety protocols at their organization. But they veered off course when they suggested that mediators codify a practice of extra fear when encountering certain vulnerable groups. Instead, the best practice might be to look for potentially violent behaviors and react uniformly to these actual behaviors.

As part of my process in writing this book, I contacted ACR in 2021 to alert them to these issues, and they placed the guidelines under review with the intent to address this problem. Hopefully, future editions of these guidelines will rectify this mistake by creating tools to respond to specific observed behaviors rather than making assumptions regarding entire classes of people. They could even use the tools in chapter 9 to help them do so.

TAKEAWAY

Any policies that profile people based on an identity characteristic, such as the presence of mental health conditions, are stigmatizing. It is better to create policies based on behaviors.

D. SCAPEGOATING

In addition to the assumptions, paternalism, and stigma that affect peoples' attitudes and ideas about mental health, these concerns also can lead to scapegoating. In every facet of our society, people and institutions single out "difficult people" or those dealing with mental health conditions to shift focus from larger problems. We have already discussed how these kinds of labels add to the stigma associated with mental health conditions. This section also shares one possible reason why this stigmatization happens in the first place: people are using mental health concerns as a proxy for not being prepared for challenging situations unrelated to mental illness.

In many areas of life, people end up doing this kind of profiling anyway. This is because it is simpler to say "watch out for people who are drunk or have a mental illness" than it is to develop robust, consistent behavior-based policies for challenging behaviors. Many challenging behavior policies and trainings inappropriately link challenging behaviors to mental illness for this reason. The solution is to create better behavior policies, as we will cover in chapter 9.

Another type of scapegoating is assuming that our practices work well for most people except those with special needs. In the case of conflict resolution practitioners, many of them believe in "following the heat" during a mediation session. This means allowing the emotions to run high and the conflict to escalate so that people are able to work through tough issues. However, many of these practitioners worry that this is not a good practice for someone with a mental health problem. What if that person gets triggered into a breakdown of some kind? What if they are too fragile to participate?

Of course, nobody would like to suddenly discover that they have to have an intense conversation instead of having the conflict resolution professional work to deescalate things. That means anyone could experience some kind of displeasure or, worse, a breakdown, if they are put through that. Instead of just wondering what could go wrong if someone has special disability needs, we should be developing our practice to prevent problems for anyone. This is called accessibility, which we cover in chapter 8. In the case of a practitioner who has decided to "follow the heat" and welcome escalation as part of their conflict resolution norms, the simple way to be accessible is to warn all parties you will do this and give them a chance to opt out.

TAKEAWAY

Sometimes people are not prepared for challenging behaviors or accessibility needs, and they end up believing that the problem is people who may have extra needs, such as people with mental illness. It is best to develop practices for responding to these challenging situations rather than scapegoating specific types of people.

i. Family Case Study: Blaming Mental Health Problems Instead of Addressing Stress

One common type of conflict in families occurs when people scapegoat someone for having mental health problems when these problems may actually be triggered or exacerbated by stressful dynamics in the family. In these cases, there are often two sides in the conflict talking past each other. Family member supporters frequently insist that their loved one has a mental health problem and needs help, whereas the loved one often insists the real problem is the stress in their family. Both perspectives are often true at the same time and in varying degrees. Yes, the loved one is triggered by real stress that needs to be addressed in some way so that the environment is not as toxic. But it may also be true that the loved one's reactions escalate beyond their normal range, which perhaps means there is a problem on that side too.

Unfortunately, when the scapegoating happens, a resolvable conflict can quickly deteriorate. The family member supporters may fear that, if they agree they are creating stress, they will end up walking on eggshells around their loved one forever. They often do not feel it's right to incur these escalated outbursts in response to the stress. On the other side, the loved one can often feel that they are less stable, and they often want to talk about it in order to get support. But they too are scared—scared that if their family blames everything on their mental health problem, then the stress will never get fixed. Even worse, they may end up getting excessive mental health treatment to cope with problems that could have been reduced if their family members had worked with them.

Too often, this situation will deteriorate into name-calling and blaming instead of connecting. This tension can be reduced or avoided entirely if everyone resists scapegoating the mental health problem for the challenging behaviors they are experiencing.

TAKEAWAY

Scapegoating is dangerous. When people blame someone's mental health condition, it can become a big barrier to conflict resolution. It is best to stop scapegoating by expanding the conversation to broader framing of problems and remaining open-minded to many possibilities for understanding and resolving the issue.

E. MENTAL HEALTH MYTHS SCENARIOS

On a scale of 1 to 5, 1 being very uncomfortable and 5 being very comfortable, how comfortable are you with the following ways of describing a mental health problem?

Chemical imbalance   _____

Mental illness   _____

Brain disorder   _____

Psychiatric disability   _____

Mad gift   _____

On a scale of 1 to 5, 1 being very uncomfortable and 5 being very comfortable, how comfortable are you with the following ways of describing a person who has a mental health problem?

Lunatic   _____

Crazy   _____

Patient   _____

Client   _____

Peer   _____

Consumer   _____

Mentally ill   _____

Psychiatric survivor   _____

Individual   _____

Highly sensitive person   _____

Abnormal   _____

For each of the labels above, ask yourself the following questions:

- What assumptions do I have about a person with this label?
- What kind of help do I assume a person with this label may need?
- What kinds of stigmatizing attitudes have I seen associated with this label?
- What kinds of problems do I blame on people with this label?

CHAPTER 4

DO WE NEED TO LABEL PEOPLE?

One myth about mental health problems is that, in order to help someone, we need to figure out the proper label for their mental health condition. This chapter explores when and how labels can be useful, with a focus on how they can also be destructive to our conflict resolution efforts.

A. THE VALUE OF LABELS

Receiving a diagnosis can be vital to someone receiving care for their mental health condition. Many mental health professionals and advocates lobby for early intervention; that is, they advocate for people to get diagnosed and treated as soon as possible before their problems become worse.[69] Likewise, there are people who feel that pathologizing and overmedicating people dooms them to more serious problems.[70]

Mary Giliberti, the executive director of the National Alliance on Mental Illness (NAMI), has written that people suffering from schizophrenia, borderline personality disorder, dual diagnosis, depression, and obsessive-compulsive disorder can get better care if their clinicians are better equipped to label these conditions early on and link them to appropriate services.[71]

These labels can become cathartic for those who receive them. Suddenly, a lifetime of stress and problems can finally make more sense when viewed through the lens of an apt mental health diagnosis. That diagnosis becomes a passport to services, whether it is help at school, therapy and medication from a clinician, or reasonable accommodations to access opportunities at work. The diagnosis can also be a first step toward self-reflection about one's sensitivities and how they relate to other people. In many ways, that label can be a lifesaver.

Yet mental health labels also have the potential to hurt someone's life. For one, people can debate who qualifies for these labels in ways that feel dehumanizing, offensive, and disempowering. We have already discussed how social stigma can become internalized and have noted that perceiving that someone fits a label can lead to destructive assumptions, paternalism, and scapegoating. Just as a label can open up a world of support and resources, it can also be a ticket to extra burdens and pains.

---

[69] Scott, E. M., Carpenter, J. S., Iorfino, F., Cross, S. P., Hermens, D. F., White, D., . . . & Hickie, I. B. (2020). Early intervention, prevention, and prediction in mood disorders: Tracking multidimensional outcomes in young people presenting for mental health care. In *Personalized Psychiatry* (pp. 39–62). Academic Press.

[70] Doblyte., S. (2020). Under-or overtreatment of mental distress? Practices, consequences, and resistance in the field of mental health care. *Qualitative Health Research, 30*(10), 1503–1516.

[71] Giliberti, Mary (2017). The importance of getting the right treatment for you. Retrieved from https://www.nami.org/Blogs/From-the-CEO/October-2017/The-Importance-of-Getting-the-Right-Treatment-for.

This is why it is important to remember that our role is not to label someone, but rather to respect their decisions and beliefs about mental health labels that affect them.

It's helpful to think of labels as decisions rather than as facts. People decide to create labels, they choose how to apply them, and they determine how to react to them. They also decide what they believe about them. It is our responsibility to listen to each person in conflict and to follow their lead so that they are empowered to share their own voice rather than react with our own interpretation about what a label might mean about their mental health needs.

TAKEAWAY

Whether labels end up being helpful or hurtful to people, it is not our role to be part of that process. Our role is to focus on the decisions people make regarding labels and follow their lead.

i. Personal Story: How Labels Can Hurt

Being open about my mental illness has frequently led to disempowering, hurtful experiences. I will never forget delivering my first presentation at an American Bar Association conference. Several people approached me afterward about hiring me to train judges and the military. I felt happy that this work was resonating. Then someone else spoke to me, and I mentioned my wife in the conversation. This person said, "Wow, she must be a very special person to take you on."

This person meant to compliment my wife, but it was also clear that they had given a heaviness to my disclosed label of bipolar disorder. Nothing about my presentation was meant to suggest it would be difficult for my wife to be with me. This person brought that stigma to the table all on their own.

Another time, years earlier, I fielded a number of offensive comments from a variety of school administrators solely because of my bipolar label. When I spoke about giving a presentation at one high school, the assistant principal told me that I had better reassure the principal that if I planned to talk about my bipolar disorder as part of the mental health presentation that I would also share that there was a "rainbow at the end of the story." This comment again showed that my label alone was seen very negatively. At a different school, I was told to be firm with the students, so I followed their procedures for maintaining their attention. A vice principal told me the students had said to her, "we can see why he has bipolar disorder because he reacted when we would not pay attention." I said I thought I was doing what I had been told, to which the vice principal replied, "Oh yeah, you were—we tell our teachers to act like they are bipolar with the students so they know they cannot get away with things."

Sadly, these examples are commonplace throughout my life, as they are for many people living with mental health problems. The second someone hears a label, their brain links it to their image of what it means for someone to have a mental illness. Frustrated students link their frustrations to the labels. Conference attendees assume their negative stereotypes of what it means for someone to live with bipolar disorder. Nervous administrative personnel worry that hearing from someone with bipolar disorder will be a burdensome story and they insist on happy endings.

As a conflict resolver, when I first started telling people in my professional community about my mental health history, people I knew started seeing me differently. I will never forget one fellow mediator's reaction when I told him my diagnosis. I had known him for years, and he just looked at me and made an awkward smile. "Wow, you're doing so well," he lilted with an over-the-top enthusiasm.

He was impressed that I had seemed normal to him, contrary to whatever stigmatizing ideas he associated with the label.

B. HOW LABELS CONFUSE DOCTORS

Differentiating between an actual mental health problem and psychiatric symptoms triggered by physical conditions can be very challenging, even for a clinician. In the realm of depression, there are a wide variety of potential medical causes for symptoms such as autoimmune diseases (e.g., lupus or arthritis), cancer (e.g., brain or lung cancer), central nervous system diseases (e.g., Parkinson's or Huntington's disease), endocrine diseases (e.g., thyroid or pituitary problems), intoxication (e.g., lead poisoning), occult infection (e.g., liver), and viral infections (e.g., influenza).[72] Similarly, psychosis can be triggered by endocrine diseases (e.g.,. Cushing's syndrome), metabolic disorders (e.g., acute intermittent porphyria), autoimmune diseases (e.g., Hashimoto encephalopathy), infections (e.g., cerebral malaria), narcolepsy, seizures, brain tumors, strokes, head injury, and more.[73] In the elderly, somewhat similar medical problems can be masked as anxiety.[74] The fact that experts are often confused about what is going on demonstrates how labels can cause problems. Knowing that psychopathology can be confused with physical conditions reinforces how important it is for us to focus on the behaviors we are observing.

Entire books have been written devoted to the art of distinguishing between mental and physical conditions.[75] There is therefore no reason for us to try to be experts in this area. There is also a known problem of undiagnosed medical illness present in patients with mental disorders. Multiple studies have demonstrated that the physical conditions of people labeled with mental health problems have often been overlooked.[76] Finally, at times people have physical symptoms that go unlabeled, and are given catch-all labels instead.

---

[72] Gagnon, F (2010). Differential diagnosis of mood disorder due to a medical condition and substance-induced mood disorder. *Integrating Science and Practice, 1*(2), 5–9.

[73] Freudenreich, O. (2010). Differential diagnosis of psychotic symptoms: Medical mimics. *Psychiatric Times, 27*(12), 56–61.

[74] Marsh, C. M. (1997). Psychiatric presentations of medical illness. *Psychiatric Clinics of North America, 20*(1), 181–204.

[75] Morrison, J. R. (1997). *When psychological problems mask medical disorders: A guide for psychotherapists.* Guilford Press.

[76] Bartsch, D. A., Shern, D. L., Feinberg, L. E., Fuller, B. B., & Willett, A. B. (1990). Screening CMHC outpatients for physical illness. *Psychiatric Services, 41*(7), 786–790; Hall, R. C., Gardner, E. R., Stickney, S. K., LeCann, A. F., & Popkin, M. K. (1980). Physical illness manifesting as psychiatric disease: II. Analysis of a state hospital inpatient population. *Archives of General Psychiatry, 37*(9), 989–995; Koran, L. M., Sox, Jr, H. C., Marton, K. I., Moltzen, S., Sox, C. H., Kraemer, H. C., . . . & Chandra, S. (1989). Medical evaluation of psychiatric patients: I. Results in a

Physical symptoms are usually explained by medical causes, psychological causes, or the unknown etiology that leads to a classification as medically unexplained physical symptoms (MUPS).[77] That's right—it is a label to say there was no label.

The terminology for physical or somatic symptoms that have no known cause even after testing, workups, and referrals is inconsistent. In addition to the term *MUPS*, people may also be labeled with somatoform disorder, functional syndromes, or somatization.[78]

Estimates of prevalence vary, ranging from as little as 11% based on a survey of doctors' recollection of how many cases of MUPS they had in the previous day, to as much as 67% of referrals to specialty clinics based on research reviewing charts.[79,80] There are signs of bias as to who gets diagnosed with the MUPS catch-all label. One study revealed that doctor dissatisfaction with the patient encounter was the stronger predictor of MUPS misdiagnosis, with younger, unmarried, anxious patients who also receive disability benefits having the highest chance of being misdiagnosed with MUPS before later receiving a different diagnosis.[81] In other words, we have clear evidence that labels are biased.

There is debate as to how MUPS should be integrated into medical practice. Some feel that the mind–body distinction is artificial. They argue that the medical community should steer away from strict application of the medical model that begets MUPS and yield to a biopsychosocial paradigm, which will better integrate these complex illness experiences.[82] Others argue that the variety of terminologies surrounding MUPS position them as something "other" than physical and cast a negative connotation on the psychological dimension of these symptoms.[83] Put simply, these labels can hurt.

The diagnostic process is imperfect even for experts, and it is especially confusing when doctors have to distinguish between physical and mental symptoms. Some argue that there should be no line between them. While this is a challenging process, two clear themes emerge. First, clinicians must be educated in the plethora of possibilities and build systems into their diagnostic process to consider, and reconsider, those possibilities on a routine basis. Second, the patient–clinician encounter is important, and more correct diagnoses emerge when clinicians build stronger relationships with their patients, listening to their voices instead of dismissing complaints as psychological and ascribing a negative connotation to psychological complaints.

---

state mental health system. *Archives of General Psychiatry, 46*(8), 733; Koranyi, E. K. (1979). Morbidity and rate of undiagnosed physical illnesses in a psychiatric clinic population. *Archives of General Psychiatry, 36*(4), 414.

[77] Huang, H., & McCarron, R. M. (2011). Medically unexplained physical symptoms: Evidence-based interventions. *Current Psychiatry, 10*(7), 17.

[78] Ibid.

[79] Swanson, L. M., Hamilton J. C., & Feldman, M. D. (2010). Physician-based estimates of medically unexplained symptoms: A comparison of four case definitions. *Family Practice, 27*(5), 487–493.

[80] Huang, H., & McCarron, R. M. (2011). Medically unexplained physical symptoms: Evidence-based interventions. *Current Psychiatry, 10*(7), 17.

[81] Nimnuan, C., Hotopf, M., & Wessely, S. (2000). Medically unexplained symptoms: How often and why are they missed? *QJM, 93*(1), 21–28.

[82] Soler, J. K., & Okkes, I. (2012). Reasons for encounter and symptom diagnoses: A superior description of patients' problems in contrast to medically unexplained symptoms (MUS). *Family Practice, 29*(3), 272–282.

[83] Greco, M. (2012). The classification and nomenclature of 'medically unexplained symptoms': Conflict, performativity and critique. *Social Science and Medicine, 75*(12), 2362–2369.

If even the experts have fraught experiences working with labels, and they know that they need to do more to listen to their patients, then it should be easy to realize that we need to do the same in our conflicts.

TAKEAWAY

Labels are imperfect, and they can disorient us or confuse a situation. Keep an open mind, listen, and trust people's choices instead of relying on labels.

C. HOW LABELING UNDERMINES CONFLICT RESOLUTION

Conflict resolution best practices dictate that mediators have an ethical obligation to be free from favoritism, bias, or prejudice and to avoid behaving in a way that appears to show partiality.[84] Using a label, or even reacting to one, may undermine this principle and become destructive to the conflict resolution process, which hinges on people believing that the process is fair. If that labeling is done without the consent or awareness of the party, then it is undermining the core mediation value of self-determination as well.

Even if you are not duty-bound as a professional conflict resolver, it is still important to respect the other person's choices in a conflict and to appeal to some sense of fairness. These tactics can facilitate a sense of empowerment, which can become a foundation for dialogue and then later agreement.

TAKEAWAY

Labeling compromises impartiality and self-determination.

---

[84] American Bar Association, American Arbitration Association, and the Association for Conflict Resolution. (2005). Model Standards of Conduct for Mediators. https://www.americanbar.org/content/dam/aba/migrated/2011_build/dispute_resolution/model_standards_conduct_april2007.authcheckdam.pdf.

D. LABEL SCENARIOS

You may come across many different kinds of labels in the world of mental health needs. Below is a list of some types of labels. For each of them, answer the following questions, imagining that someone in the conflict has used this term:

- What is okay to say about this label?

- What should I not say about this label?

- How will I know if this label is helpful to know in this conflict?

- How can I prevent this label from becoming destructive?

Labels

- High-functioning

- Euthymic

- Living with a disability

- Living with a mental health problem

- In crisis

- Low-functioning

- Dysphoric

- Distressed

- Well-managed

CHAPTER 5

DO PEOPLE WITH MENTAL HEALTH PROBLEMS NEED SPECIAL HELP?

Another myth surrounding mental health problems is that someone who is living with such a problem needs special help. This is confusing because the law, through the ADA, actually says that many businesses and public organizations do owe a responsibility to provide adjustments for someone with a disability as long as the request is not an undue hardship or something that creates a safety risk for others.

Yet, just because people with disabilities have that right to request special assistance does not mean it is right for us to assume that someone we believe has a disability might need our help. Historically, assuming someone with a disability may require assistance has been known as a common stereotype. This type of assumption is the source of many paternalistic microaggressions and acts of discrimination. A 2010 study of disability microaggressions by Keller and Galgay shows the harmful effects of well-intentioned, but inappropriate inquiries:[85]

- "Targets did not see these 'well-intentioned' efforts as harmless but as examples of the insensitivity of the perpetrators, their lack of attention to boundaries, and their lack of concern for the cost to the target in losing control of their personal information." (Keller & Galgay, 2010, p. 252).

- "While targets seemed to acknowledge these misguided offers of assistance to most likely represent a genuine intent to be helpful on the part of the perpetrator, the aggregate impact of continuous unsolicited, unwanted, and unneeded offers of help was reported to be overwhelmingly negative, intense, and long lasting." (Keller & Galgay, 2010, p.253).

Beyond the negative impact of these invasive offers of help, it is also against the law to engage in unnecessary inquiries. Thus, if we act on the myth that all people with mental health problems might need us to check if they need special help, we could end up running afoul of the ADA's prohibitions regarding unnecessary inquiries and examinations.

The ADA explicitly acknowledges that unnecessary inquiries about someone's disability, including their mental health condition, are inappropriate and can amount to discrimination. Very often, we hear this issue discussed in the context of preemployment job offers or in rules about when it is appropriate to

---

[85] Keller, R. M., & Galgay, C. E. (2010). Microaggressive experiences of people with disabilities. In D. W. Sue (Ed.), *Microaggressions and marginality: Manifestation, dynamics, and impact* (pp. 241–267). John Wiley.

perform medical examinations as part of the job once someone has been hired. There have even been big debates about whether this is appropriate in the context of incentivized workplace wellness programs that require the revelation of some private medical data for participation. These types of inquiries are covered for employers under Title I of the ADA, but for mediators the relevant provisions are typically Title III as related to public accommodations—places that are open to the public. Public accommodations are places serving a customer or service-user rather than hiring the person as an employee. The ADA Title III Technical Assistance Manual broadly prohibits unnecessary inquiries (III-4.1300), and § 36.302(c)(6) makes clear the prohibitions against making inquiries to someone with a service animal beyond asking generally if it is required due to a disability and what tasks it has been trained to perform.[86] There are similar regulations about what questions can be asked to a ticketing agent when someone buys an accessible seating option (§ 36.302(f)(2)) or about questions regarding a wheelchair or power-driven mobility device (§ 36.311(c)). The general rule of thumb is to avoid asking any unnecessary questions about someone's disability.

For some additional helpful context, there is the guidance that the Equal Employment Opportunity Commission (EEOC) has provided for understanding employer responsibilities under the ADA.[87] The EEOC specifically explains that it is the employee's responsibility to ask for the reasonable accommodation, even in cases where the disability is known to the employer. According to the EEOC, the employer may take steps to inquire if an accommodation is needed when the employer has a reasonable basis to believe that the employee with the disability might need an accommodation and that they might be unable to ask for it. In other words, these inquiries should be avoided as a general practice.

To understand the implications of some of these ADA violations regarding unnecessary inquiries, it is helpful to review some of the publicly posted ADA Enforcement Actions. An example settlement is the 2019 Wildwood Inn Settlement Agreement which resolved a case in which a military veteran with posttraumatic stress disorder (PTSD) received inappropriate inquiries about their service animal.[88] As part of the settlement, Wildwood Inn agreed to implement a service animal policy, train their staff, and keep records of the training for review by the United States Attorney's Office.

Related enforcement actions shed light on how the ADA protects people from being screened into different categories based on misuse of information learned through inquiries. The Alliance Health and Human Services Settlement Agreement was in response to individuals being denied admission to skilled nursing facilities following patient disclosures that they were taking medications used to treat opioid use disorder (OUD).[89] The agreement included the implementation of a new nondiscrimination policy, staff training about Title III of the ADA and how it applies to OUD, and logging to ensure patients were

---

[86] Department of Justice (2010). Americans with Disabilities Act Title III Regulations: Nondiscrimination on the Basis of Disability by Public Accommodations and in Commercial Facilities. Retrieved from https://www.ada.gov/regs2010/titleIII_2010/titleIII_2010_regulations.pdf.

[87] Equal Employment Opportunity Commission (2002). Enforcement Guidance on Reasonable Accommodation and Undue Hardship under the ADA. Retrieved from https://www.eeoc.gov/laws/guidance/enforcement-guidance-reasonable-accommodation-and-undue-hardship-under-ada.

[88] Settlement Agreement between the United States of America and Divyalakshmi Inc. under the Americans with Disabilities Act (2019). Retrieved from https://www.ada.gov/divyalakshmi_wildwood_sa.html.

[89] Settlement Agreement between the United States of America and Alliance Health and Human Services (2020). Retrieved from https://www.ada.gov/aahs_sa.html.

not turned away in the future based on inappropriate screening and eligibility criteria, along with a financial penalty. A 2014 settlement agreement with Quinnipiac University determined that it discriminated against a student by placing her on mandatory leave of absence due to her depression rather than explore modifying their leave policy to allow her to continue her coursework.[90]

In interpreting the ADA's provisions regarding disability-related inquiries, the EEOC has also provided clear guidance defining what kinds of inquiries are and are not prohibited.[91] The EEOC describes a disability-related inquiry as any question or set of questions likely to elicit information about a disability. This might include asking someone whether they have a disability, what is the cause of a known or perceived disability, or what is the nature or severity of a disability. It may mean requesting medical documentation, genetic information, or workers compensation history among other possible questions. It could be broad questions about possible impairments or questions about whether a person takes any medications or drugs. Examples of permitted questions that are not considered disability inquiries include general well-being questions like "how are you" or requests for a contact in case of a medical emergency.

According to the EEOC, the ADA prohibits all disability-related inquiries before employment and allows inquiries once someone starts work only if those inquiries are job-related and consistent with business necessity. Even when an employee requests a reasonable accommodation, the documentation and information the employee must provide are limited to whatever is necessary to establish the nature, severity, and duration of the impairment and the basis for the requested accommodation. The person's request for a reasonable accommodation does not allow the employer to have broad access to unrelated documentation. Running throughout the ADA and its implementing regulations is a common theme of protecting people from inappropriate inquiries about their disabilities.

This protection from inquiries also applies to psychological testing. While some kinds of personality testing are still potentially okay, there have been cases that define psychological tests as inappropriate medical examinations under the ADA, such as *Karraker v. Rent-A-Center*.[92] Rent-A-Center was using the Minnesota Multiphasic Personality Inventory (MMPI) to screen out candidates from consideration for management positions. The court concluded that this test could be used to weed out people with certain disorders even though it did not directly test for them, and it was deemed inappropriate.

These are a few facets of many complicated layers of how the ADA handles disability inquiries. The general thrust is that any questions that may lead someone to reveal the nature and severity of a known disability, or the existence of a disability that has been unknown, are potential violations of the ADA regulations and case law protecting people from unnecessary inquiries across a variety of areas. While these questions are often seen as a necessary or appropriate part of the process of providing a reasonable accommodation, as part of checking that someone is able to perform the essential functions of a job they already have, or as part of an individualized examination to see if that person may amount to a "direct

---

[90] Settlement Agreement between the United States of America and Quinnipiac University (2014). Retrieved from https://www.ada.gov/quinnipiac_sa.htm.

[91] Equal Employment Opportunity Commission (2000). Enforcement Guidance on Disability-Related Inquiries and Medical Examinations of Employees under the ADA. Retrieved from https://www.eeoc.gov/laws/guidance/enforcement-guidance-disability-related-inquiries-and-medical-examinations-employees.

[92] Karraker v. Rent-A-Center, Inc., 411 F.3d 831 (7th Cir. 2005).

threat" to the health and safety of others in that environment, still a best practice is to avoid asking any questions unless they become necessary.

So, what does all of this legal background mean when it comes to assuming someone with a mental health problem might need our help? It is reasonable to wonder if someone needs help when they are experiencing a mental health need or a diagnosable mental health problem. After all, these kinds of difficult feelings or diagnosable conditions correspond to real deficits. People often need to do things to cope or to get treatment for mental disorders. They may need to take time off from work or school and to pursue inpatient treatment in some cases. Therefore, it might not seem like it is really a myth that people need special help for mental health problems. We know they have a legal right to help, and we know treatments are available. Where is the myth?

The myth is that this person in front of you right now needs the help now; that it is okay to assume a need based on their condition; and that you are entitled to talk to them about it.

The reality is that it is possible that anyone *might* need help at any time, that you have no business assuming anyone specifically needs that help, and that you should not single anyone out to offer it.

Instead of believing it is our responsibility to assume someone needs help and to offer it, we should focus on being ready to provide help when asked and otherwise on improving our general processes. Help should be readily available for all people who need it, not just the people we believe are presenting with mental health situations. This help is called accessibility, and it is covered in chapter 8.

TAKEAWAY

While it is good to be aware that anyone you are engaging with during a conflict may need help and while it is okay to generally offer resources for everyone, it is wrong to assume that someone specific needs help—especially in relation to their having a mental health condition.

i. Personal Story: A University Suggesting a Long Medical Leave

I was first diagnosed with bipolar disorder after I was surprised by a manic episode at the start of my junior year of college. After not sleeping for four straight days, I wound up hospitalized in the psychiatric unit of the university hospital, and I was forced to take a medical leave of absence in order to process my recovery.

The school sent me a letter letting me know I could return the following year and shared instructions on how to do so. That would have meant a full year away from my classes and my community. You may recall from an earlier personal story that I had discovered I had a choice in care plans after visiting two potential clinicians, and I chose the one who told me I could recover and return to school after only a semester.

But how would I have known that returning in a semester was even an option, given the letter I had received suggesting I wait a year?

When I was first hospitalized, the university's counseling center director pulled my family aside and told them that the school would try to guide me to come back in a year but that returning in a semester was possible too. Without that heads up, we would have never even understood we had the choice to pursue my return in the spring. The school was trying to make that choice for me, assuming I needed the extra help of the full year off.

But why? As I have continued my career in mental health, I have become more familiar with one reason why a school might suggest a year-long leave to their students without telling them to come back sooner. The reason is that bipolar disorder is a potentially chronic disease, with people often having relapses within the first year. Rather than having students experience those relapses on campus, the schools might prefer to wait and see if the student is stable or not during that full year away.

This approach is problematic not just because of the paternalism involved, but also because each semester away from school has real costs. Friends grow apart, timelines for graduation change, and the climate at home may not be comfortable. Lucky for me, the counseling director had helped my family understand our options, so the school was unable to guide me into the longer timeline they had suggested.

A. WHY OFFERING HELP CAN BE PATERNALISTIC

Offering unrequested help is not just potentially discriminatory, but it can also be paternalistic. Any tone that we know better than the person, that we can tell they need help that they did not bring up themselves—this is a tone that reflects our own biases, and it is a tone that overrides the person's autonomy.

This is the shortest section in the book because it is such a simple principle.

TAKEAWAY

Deciding help for another person strips them of their autonomy. Keep them in the driver's seat; share options with them and let them choose and offer those options consistently to everyone.

B. CAPACITY TO MAKE DECISIONS

One common misconception about mental health problems is that people living with them lack the capacity to make their own decisions. Many professional conflict resolvers erroneously believe they have to perform a capacity assessment just because they hear a person has a mental health diagnosis.

Because capacity is so essential to functioning in a conflict, I am including some research about capacity assessments to help demonstrate their usefulness as well as their limitations:

Interpretations of various legal doctrines related to the rights of people with mental disorders can vary with popular sentiment and sensationalized media coverage.[93] Although these stereotypes increase the salience of the capacity question when a mental disorder is mentioned, the reality is that capacity assessments are vague procedures that may, in general practice, violate ADR principles of neutrality. For instance, a review of 66 studies of surrogate decision making among medical professionals found that the decision-making process was often prompted by "gut feelings" something was wrong as opposed to defined cutoffs indicating problems had escalated to a point necessitating overriding patient autonomy and administering an intervention.[94] Moreover, although these decisions tended to be aimed at quality of life, different people used different definitions of that term. This implies human bias in these clinical decisions.

Before deciding when a conflict resolution session would not be appropriate in mental health contexts due to lack of capacity, it is important to fully understand what mental health capacity assessments entail. The term *competency* is the result of a legal determination, while the term *capacity* reflects clinical standards.[95] Most state laws define incompetency as requiring some kind of disease and disorder, along with a cognitive or psychiatric deficit that leads to functional inabilities that exceed an acceptable risk to that person or society as determined by an expert.[96]

Legal competency standards regarding functional abilities have led experts to develop criteria of four functional abilities for assessing capacity: understanding, appreciation, reasoning, and expression of choice.[97] Rather than conduct a single generalized capacity assessment, modern practice dictates that the assessment be performed in relation to specific decisions.[98]

There is no gold standard in capacity instruments,[99] but the MacArthur Competence Assessment Tool for Treatment (MacCAT-T) is the most heavily validated and frequently used tool and for some it is considered to be a gold standard.[100] Others argue that additional criteria must be added; for instance, that the expressed choice be based on criteria that are reasonable to others.[101]

---

[93] Cannistraro, T. (2009). A call for minds: The unknown extent of societal influence on the legal rights of involuntarily and voluntarily committed mental health patients. *Annals of Health Law, 19,* 425.

[94] Clarke, G., Harrison, K., Holland, A., Kuhn, I., & Barclay, S. (2013). How are treatment decisions made about artificial nutrition for individuals at risk of lacking capacity? A systematic literature review. *PloS one, 8*(4), e61475.

[95] Palmer, B. W., & Savla, G. N. (2007). The association of specific neuropsychological deficits with capacity to consent to research or treatment. *Journal of the International Neuropsychological Society, 13*(06), 1047–1059.

[96] Sabatino, C. P., & Basingelr, J. S. L. (2000). Competency: Reforming our legal fictions. *Journal of Mental Health and Aging, 6,* 2.

[97] Moye, J., Gurrera, R. J., Karel, M. J., Edelstein, B., & O'Connell, C. (2006). Empirical advances in the assessment of the capacity to consent to medical treatment: Clinical implications and research needs. *Clinical Psychology Review, 26*(8), 1054–1077.

[98] Candia, P. C., & Barba, A. C. (2011). Mental capacity and consent to treatment in psychiatric patients: The state of the research. *Current Opinion in Psychiatry, 24*(5), 442–446.

[99] Banner, N. F. (2012). Unreasonable reasons: Normative judgements in the assessment of mental capacity. *Journal of Evaluation in Clinical Practice, 18*(5), 1038–1044.

[100] Howe, E. (2009). Ethical aspects of evaluating a patient's mental capacity. *Psychiatry, 6*(7), 15.

[101] Chariand, Louis C. (2001). "Mental competence and value: The problem of normativity in the assessment of decision-making capacity." *Psychiatry, Psychology and Law, 8*(2), 135–145.

A systematic review of 37 papers from 1967 to 2006 found 29 different capacity instruments.[102] These instruments relied on a variety of techniques, including asking patients to answer questions about hypothetical vignettes or asking direct questions. Some of the questions focused on specific procedures and others were flexible to a wide range of treatment decisions.[103]

These capacity tests are considered to be too limited to stand alone, and so they are often used in conjunction with other criteria as part of clinical judgment, such as ability to execute life tasks. Some suggest the tools are most necessary when people seem to have ambiguous capacity, as opposed to using them routinely as a matter of course.[104] Different clinicians reach different conclusions about capacity. A study of 111 nurses who were asked questions based on the MacCAT-T showed a range of opinions about whether a specific case example was competent.[105]

Most often clinicians tend to question capacity when the patient disagrees with clinical advice, rather than asking before the time of consent.[106] Some suggest that this may explain why involuntarily admitted patients are more likely to lack capacity.[107] This idea that capacity assessments tend to be differentially applied is troubling. When these assessments are used as a tool to override disagreeing patients rather than protect those who might be acquiescing, it is a sign that they are augmenting power imbalances rather than supporting self-determination.

Capacity assessments are flawed even when mental health experts are administering them. Perhaps mediators are best advised to leave those assessments to the professionals and instead focus on validating the perspective of any party they meet without auditing capacity.

TAKEAWAY

Even the most rigorous capacity assessments are flawed and are used in a biased manner, with people often questioning the capacity of people who disagree with them. Be very careful when assuming anyone lacks the capacity to make their own decisions.

---

[102] Okai, D., Owen, G., McGuire, H., Singh, S., Churchill, R., & Hotopf, M. (2007). Mental capacity in psychiatric patients: Systematic review. *British Journal of Psychiatry, 191*(4), 291–297.

[103] Ibid.

[104] Sturman, E. D. (2005). The capacity to consent to treatment and research: A review of standardized assessment tools. *Clinical Psychology Review, 25*(7), 954–974.

[105] Sehiralti, M., & Rahime, A. E. (2013). Decisions of psychiatric nurses about duty to warn, compulsory hospitalization, and competence of patients. *Nursing Ethics, 20*(1), 41–50.

[106] Jones, R. C., & Holden, T. (2004). A guide to assessing decision-making capacity. *Cleveland Clinic Journal of Medicine, 71*(12), 971–975; Wong, J. G., Cheung, E. P., & Chen, E. Y. (2005). Decision-making capacity of inpatients with schizophrenia in Hong Kong. *Journal of Nervous and Mental Disease, 193*(5), 316–322.; Bean, G., Nishisato, S., Rector, N. A., & Glancy, G. (1996). The assessment of competence to make a treatment decision: An empirical approach. *Canadian Journal of Psychiatry. Revue canadienne de psychiatrie, 41*(2), 85–92.

[107] Okai, McGuire, Singh, Churchill, and Hotopf. Mental capacity in psychiatric patients: Systematic review.

C. WHY ALL PARTIES DESERVE HELP

Mental health needs are universal and on a spectrum. Rather than assume we can guess who needs help based on the labels they have associated with them or our own assessment of their mental health needs, we must remember that everyone has mental health needs.

Conflicts are challenging for anyone, and we all have bad days when we may experience diminished capacity just because of the stress of the conflict, apart from any mental health condition. That is why we should stop looking for people who may have disqualifying deficits and instead focus on supporting everyone in a conflict. We can move from determining capacity to facilitating competencies.[108]

This consideration is important in any conflict, and we must always remember our own needs and limits as well. People are not purely rational, static actors. Everyone has feelings and fluctuations, and everyone can use support. Moreover, we never know who might need it, when they might need it, and why. There are people who may not have serious mental health needs. but they feel comfortable asserting themselves, and others who may have very serious needs that they keep to themselves. There are folks who would consider making a request for a reasonable accommodation for a disability, and others who would never want to do that but might respond to a general offer to adjust our process.

We look at ways to offer these kinds of supportive adjustments in chapter 8.

TAKEAWAY

Everyone can benefit from help, and it is easiest for them to get it if we make broad, general offers of support to everyone in a conflict instead of trying to guess who might need assistance

D. HELP SCENARIOS

Think about the following questions for reflection:

- How can I offer help to people who might need it without discriminating?

- When is it appropriate for me to offer them help?

- Who needs my help?

- What kinds of process adjustments can I make during a conflict?

---

[108] Crawford, S. H., Dabney, L., Filner, J. M., & Maida, P. R. (2003). From determining capacity to facilitating competencies: A new mediation framework. *Conflict Resolution Quarterly, 20*(4), 385–401.

CHAPTER 6

DO PEOPLE WITH MENTAL HEALTH PROBLEMS EXHIBIT CHALLENGING BEHAVIORS?

The last big myth we will debunk about mental health problems is the idea that the presence of a mental health problem carries with it some risk of challenging behavior, be it violence or a disconnect or general disruptions. This chapter discusses the history of these associations and shows why developing practices that assume this link is not only ineffective but also undermines the conflict resolution process.

A. DEBUNKING THE RISK OF HARM ASSUMPTION

Assessment for risk of harm has origins in the once-common assumption that people with certain mental disorders were "dangerous." This global assessment has been rejected as unsupported by empirical evidence and perpetuating stigma against people with psychiatric illnesses.[109] Data shows an increase in the number of people who reported viewing those with mental illness as violent between 1950 and 1996. This suggests that the increased usage of the phrase "danger to self or others" as part of the dangerousness standard for involuntary commitment laws permeated public perception resulting in more stigma associating violence with mental illness.[110] Today, the idea that certain mental illnesses are persistently and invariably associated with violence has been discredited. As a result, clinicians are instead focusing on specific circumstances that lead to risk of violence.[111]

Evaluating potential for violence is now captured under the construct of risk assessment. Many tools are available to assess risk for violence; the scores on these instruments can result in overriding patient autonomy by subjecting patients to involuntary hospitalization, forced medication, and other coercive measures.[112] These instruments are not foolproof by any means. It is expected that the screener will have false negatives as well as false positives, which can stigmatize large groups of people erroneously labeled at high risk for violence.[113] Moreover, because serious violence is rare and there are no highly effective

---

[109] Phelan, J. C., & Link, B. G. (1998). The growing belief that people with mental illnesses are violent: The role of the dangerousness criterion for civil commitment. *Social Psychiatry and Psychiatric Epidemiology, 33*(1), S7–S12.

[110] Ibid.

[111] Harris, A., & Lurigio, A. J. (2007). Mental illness and violence: A brief review of research and assessment strategies. *Aggression and Violent Behavior, 12*(5), 542–551.

[112] Laiho, T., Kattainen, E., Åstedt-Kurki, P., Putkonen, H., Lindberg, N., & Kylmä, J. (2013). Clinical decision making involved in secluding and restraining an adult psychiatric patient: An integrative literature review. *Journal of Psychiatric and Mental Health Nursing, 20*(9), 830–839.

[113] Large, M., & Mullin, K. (2011). Risk assessment and screening for violence. *European Psychiatry, 26*(2), 132.

preventative treatments, experts often suggest that screening is not worthwhile.[114] When they are used, clinical risk assessments present problems of interrater reliability. Thus, experts suggest that multiple people make assessments and that they rely on multiple sources of information of the highest possible accuracy.[115]

Despite practitioners' best efforts, these kinds of assessments are flawed. There is a long-standing idea that there is an inability of clinicians to make predictions about likelihood of violence in the long term, and such predictions can only be made in short time horizons and specific settings, such as the emergency room context.[116]

Involuntary hospitalization may happen when a determination of risk of harm to self or others is made. It is associated with the unavailability of alternatives to hospitalization,[117] referral by family or a doctor,[118] and evaluation while in a police setting or a hospital emergency room.[119] Interestingly, a study completed in 2013 showed that referral by doctors who did not know patients was correlated with a higher chance of hospitalization,[120] as was being married.[121]

The fact that hospitalization is more likely to result if the doctor is a stranger implies that doctors who know patients may be more likely to believe they are safe, reflecting some familiarity bias in these risk of harm assessments. However, other factors such as family referrals or being married may imply that having a supporter increases the likelihood of admission, perhaps because a family member or spouse seems to have implicit authority to override their loved ones' wishes not to be committed. This, too, shows the introduction of bias into these decisions.

The ameliorative impact of the availability of alternative options suggests that these risk assessment determinations are not clear-cut and are potentially used as a last resort when compared to other options.

---

[114] Ibid.

[115] Feeney, A. (2008). The principles of risk assessment. *Medicine, 36*(8), 399–401.

[116] Monahan, J. (1978). Prediction research and the emergency commitment of dangerous mentally ill persons: A reconsideration. *American Journal of Psychiatry, 135*, 198–201.

[117] McGarvey, E. L., Leon-Verdin, M., Wanchek, T. N., & Bonnie, R. J. (2013). Decisions to initiate involuntary commitment: the role of intensive community services and other factors. *Psychiatric Services, 64*(2), 120–126; Engleman, N. B., Jobes, D. A., Berman, A. L., & Langbein, L. I. (1998). Clinicians' decision making about involuntary commitment. Psychiatric Services, 49(7), 941–945.

[118] Braitman, A., Dauriac-Le Masson, V., Beghelli, F., Gallois, E., Guillibert, E., Hoang, C., . . . & Guedj, M. J. (2013). La décision d'hospitalisation sans consentement aux urgences: approche dimensionnelle ou catégorielle? [Decision of emergency involuntary hospitalization: Categorical or dimensional approach?]. *L'Encephale, 40*(3), 247–254; Hustoft, K., Larsen, T. K., Auestad, B., Joa, I., Johannessen, J. O., & Ruud, T. (2013). Predictors of involuntary hospitalizations to acute psychiatry. *International Journal of Law and Psychiatry, 36*(2), 136–143.

[119] McGarvey, Leon-Verdin, Wanchek, & Bonnie. Decisions to initiate involuntary commitment; Myklebust, L. H., Sørgaard, K., Røtvold, K., & Wynn, R. (2012). Factors of importance to involuntary admission. *Nordic Journal of Psychiatry, 66*(3), 178–182.

[120] Hustoft, et al., Predictors of involuntary hospitalizations to acute psychiatry.

[121] Braitman et al., Decision of emergency involuntary hospitalization.

TAKEAWAY

Associating dangerousness with mental health problems is fraught with error and inappropriate. Even if there were such an association, there is no unbiased or accurate way to predict this harm. Consequently, clinicians and others end up using their biased judgment to make these determinations.

i. Conflict Resolver Case Study: Screening Out Cases with Mental Illness

Once I was trained as a mediator, I began noticing that conflict resolvers showed a number of biases in their response to parties with suspected or disclosed mental health experiences. I was also involved in a research project that documented how these kinds of screening practices were codified in books and policies. Some of the reports indicated that dispute resolution professionals felt challenged about how to respond when they encountered mental health concerns.[122] In one survey of collaborative law practice reference books, many authors suggested that cases be screened out for rejection or further scrutiny if the parties had mental health problems, were taking mental health medications, were receiving disability benefits, had a history of hospitalizations, had a record of suicide attempts, had specific challenging diagnoses or "serious mental illness," or, more generally, had mental health histories of any kind.[123] This guidance to screen out parties based on mental health criteria explicitly codified unconscious bias into deliberate, inappropriate practices.

All of the various collaborative law books seemed to base their advice on the assumption that parties with mental illness may engage in dangerous, disruptive, or disconnected behaviors in which they lack capacity to participate in a mediation. As we have seen throughout this book, it is not only unethical to make these kinds of assumptions in conflict resolution but they are also unsupported by the expert evidence. Chapters 8 and 9 will teach ways to account for challenging behavior and accessibility concerns based on universal standards of behavior instead of inappropriately screening on the basis of mental health conditions.

---

[122] Cleary, J. (2015). "On the Question of a Party's Capacity to Use Mediation." *Mediate.com*. Retrieved from http://www.mediate.com/articles/ClearyJ2.cfm; Rutter, Mandy. (2014). "Mental Health and Mediation: Is Mediation Always the Right Process?" *Mediate.com*. Retrieved from http://www.mediate.com/articles/RutterMbl20140603.cfm.

[123] Lande, J., & Mosten, F. S. (2010). "Collaborative lawyers' duties to screen the appropriateness of collaborative law and obtain clients' informed consent to use collaborative law." *Ohio State Journal on Dispute Resolution, 25,* 347.

TAKEAWAY

Screening out someone from a conflict resolution process is inappropriate if it is based on them having a mental health diagnosis. Instead, any process adjustments should be based solely on objective behavior criteria.

ii. Workplace Case Study: Challenging Behavior Assumptions at Work

Employers often inappropriately tend to see people with mental illnesses as unintelligent, dangerous, unreliable, aggressive, lacking in impulse control, unreasonable, and unpredictable.[124] They might question these employees' performance and work quality as well as their skills, their social abilities, and their ability to handle work stress. This may explain why they are more willing to hire people with physical disabilities than people with mental illnesses. Russinova et al. (2011) reported the following comments from the employees they surveyed:

- "They all expected me to be violent and my boss said, "let me know if you're going to blow us all away.""

- "Another orthopedic surgeon told a doctor I was sharing the clinic with that I was 'crazy', and the doctor should not share the office with me. Fortunately, the second doctor did not listen to the stigma."

- "The worst I saw was the disrespect mental health 'professionals' displayed regarding their patients—poking fun of them behind their backs, referring to their patients using derogatory terms."

This research study is just one of many that have demonstrated the terrible assumptions people at work tend to make when they learn someone has or may have a mental health problem. These assumptions are erroneous and nonproductive.

TAKEAWAY

Workplaces are breeding grounds for all sorts of toxic and nonproductive assumptions when mental health situations arise. Instead of succumbing to these imagined backstories or profiles about a person's disclosed mental health situation, focus on developing impartial responses to observable behaviors befitting everyone's role at work.

---

[124] Russinova, Z., Griffin, S., Bloch, P., Wewiorski, N. J., & Rosoklija, I. (2011). Workplace prejudice and discrimination toward individuals with mental illnesses. *Journal of Vocational Rehabilitation, 35*(3), 227–241.

B. FAIRNESS TIPSHEET (TOOL)

The word "impartiality" means treating everyone the same way and making use of a fair process. In conflict resolution processes, a mediator might assure all parties involved that they are being listened to equally and that the mediator has no stake in the outcome. But you can still use impartiality to be empowering even if you have a different role where you do have a clear stake in the outcome (such as the well-being and safety of everyone in the school community if you work in a school, or the positive work climate if you are a manager). Infusing your processes with impartiality can help people feel empowered and respected.

▶ **Try Universal Interventions**

Treating everyone the same (e.g., sharing one universal list of resources on every encounter) can prevent bias in referrals and can help protect people from feeling they are being singled out.

▶ **Focus on Specific Behaviors, Not Generalized Labels and Diagnoses**

Don't construct a profile of someone's situation (e.g., labeling someone as "in distress," "on the verge of a nervous breakdown," "depressed"). Do discuss observable issues (e.g., observed performance). Unless your role is to make clinical assessments, avoid assessing or diagnosing someone who comes to you.

▶ **Create Objective Behavior Plans in Advance**

To demonstrate impartiality, it is helpful to create clear policies for emergencies, disruptions, and other problems in advance of any situation that may arise.

By deferring to an **objective process**, with clear roles and boundaries, conflict resolution professionals empower participants while being transparent about limitations.

▶ **Know Your Role and Boundaries**

Before you have encounters discussing mental health, think about what your role is and how you plan to operationalize it. Be aware of your comfort level and boundaries, and don't take on more responsibility than you find you are comfortable with.

▶ **Be Transparent about Your Role and the Needs of the Community**

It's okay to acknowledge that there are limitations of what you can do: always be proactively transparent about your limitations and boundaries.

▶ **Judge Your Success on Your Process, Not on Health Outcomes**

From an empowerment perspective, you're successful when you implement a process in accordance with your principles. This doesn't mean disregarding mental health outcomes. But remember that you can do all of the right things and someone can still have a bad outcome.

C. CHALLENGING BEHAVIOR SCENARIOS

A client has recently expressed feelings of being overwhelmed and is now hyperventilating and clutching their arm.

- What challenging behavior(s) do you notice, if any?
- How do you know the threshold when this becomes a problem?
- How do you know what action is appropriate to take?
- What assumptions have you been making?
- Did you already have a response planned in advance, or are you improvising?

Two people have had a number of verbal conflicts, and now one tells the other: "You'll be sorry."

- What challenging behavior(s) do you notice, if any?
- How do you know the threshold when this becomes a problem?
- How do you know what action is appropriate to take?
- What assumptions have you been making?
- Did you already have a response planned in advance, or are you improvising?

One person is calling another some vicious names.

- What challenging behavior(s) do you notice, if any?
- How do you know the threshold when this becomes a problem?
- How do you know what action is appropriate to take?
- What assumptions have you been making?
- Did you already have a response planned in advance, or are you improvising?

PART III

Best Practices for Empowerment

CHAPTER 7

TALK ABOUT MENTAL HEALTH IN AN EMPOWERING WAY

Whenever we discuss mental health, it is important we do so in a way that feels empowering toward anyone who may have a mental health condition. We have already covered the ways that assumptions, paternalism, stigma, and scapegoating can sneak into our conversations about mental health. We understand that it is therefore important to make sure that every person feels that their perspective matters, that their choices are being respected, and that they are being listened to instead of being directed.

It is usually not our place to start a conversation about a person's mental health. Sometimes, however, they will choose to talk about it with us, so it helps to be ready for those conversations. The subject could also come up in some of the other scenarios we described in chapter 2. Moreover, we may want to talk about mental health more generally to promote resources to clients or employees or family members as part of our general culture of wellness. When these situations arise, how can we be sure we are talking about mental health in empowering ways?

This chapter shares some techniques and insights designed to ensure you are using empowering language when you approach these conversations. Whether you are talking about mental health with a loved one who is seeking your support, a coworker who is disclosing a need for a reasonable accommodation, or a client who has mentioned the topic in passing, this chapter will arm you with the information you need to know in order to navigate that conversation with sensitivity, respect for self-determination, and awareness of the boundaries of your role.

TAKEAWAY

Whatever your role is, it is best to approach mental health conversations by deferring to each person's individual choices, focusing your contributions on validating their perspective and sharing objective behavior observations that are appropriate for you to comment on based on your specific role. These practices will help you empower people when you are discussing mental health.

A. PERSON-FIRST LANGUAGE

Person-first language is a best practice for talking about any kind of disability or health problem in a manner that leaves that person with a sense of dignity and individuality. Simply put, person-first language means avoiding ever defining a person by their health condition. Instead of putting those designations front and center, we emphasize that people are just that—people.

In practice, this means a simple yet profound shift: Instead of calling someone an "addict," call them a "person in recovery from a substance use condition." Instead of saying, "Dan is bipolar," say that "Dan has bipolar disorder."

The idea is to avoid offending or disempowering anyone by making them feel labeled by their condition. You can do this with any label, including disability labels. Pay careful attention not to call someone "disabled" instead of a "person living with a disability." Avoid using adjectives like "schizophrenic," whether you are describing a person or anything else (sometimes these conditions are used nonclinically as metaphors in everyday speech). It may take some practice, and it is often easier to notice in writing, but it is helpful to build this habit to avoid offending people.

TAKEAWAY

Use person-first language instead of defining a person by their mental health condition.

i. Personal Story: Identity-First Language

As we have seen, it can be challenging to figure out the right thing to say about mental health, and different communities have different responses. In my line of work, there has been a learning curve as I have encountered different groups who preferred the words "peer," "consumer," "survivor," and so on—some of the varying terminologies we explored in chapter 1.

During one week, I kept using the wrong terms for different communities I had spoken with. I tried the word "consumer" with a support group, and someone said, "I don't like the term consumer—I'm not shopping for detergent." I used the word "peer" in another context, and no one knew what I meant. I consulted an expert to shop around my idea to use the phrase "mental health needs," and she said she objected to the entire conception of mental health. She preferred to think of people as having an emotional health that is not localized to the brain.

*Finally, I was delivering a conference workshop at a NAMI event, sharing insights from a school mental health awareness program when a woman raised her hand and corrected the language I had used to describe myself. "You said it wrong," she said. "You said you **are** bipolar, when really you should say you **have** bipolar disorder."*

I replied that I had bipolar disorder, and so I could describe my condition however I wanted. I then shared some more information. Yes, there is such a thing as person-first language, I remarked, which is important to use for describing someone else's experience, and yes, plenty of people get of-

fended when anyone shifts out of that kind of phrasing. There are people who are very firm in those beliefs, who say "I would not say, 'I am cancer' so why would I ever say, 'I am bipolar?'"

That is all true. However, I often say, "I am tall" and nobody gets offended.

Though I respect person-first language and I model it in my training programs, in my personal life I am comfortable occasionally saying "I am bipolar" because it is part of how I construct my personal identity. Through all of the open-mindedness I share about labels, and all of the personal misgivings that I have about this one, sometimes I still end up saying "I am bipolar."

The moral of the story? It is always best to use person-first language to discuss someone else's experiences, but it is also best not to contradict someone's own language for describing their own experiences.

Some people choose to identify with certain attributes, and this is considered identity-first language. If someone chooses to identify with this kind of language, they should not be corrected when they talk about their own experience.

B. DON'T ASSUME; ASK!

As we've seen, assumptions are dangerous. With all of that as a foundation, what is the best thing for us to actually do? We must always be on guard to resist all assumptions. Instead, we need to ask questions. That sounds simpler than it is. What if we ask the wrong questions? What if we inadvertently start letting our assumptions run the show because we are assuming we need to ask questions that are actually inappropriate?

First, the question of when to ask questions is easily answered: You should only discuss mental health needs when someone brings their needs up to you. As we have discussed, many people have trouble with this notion because they believe that it is important to check in with someone about mental health concerns. But that is never our role: our role, rather, is to discuss the behavior that is relevant to us, in open-ended ways, and to be ready if the topic of mental health needs arises. For instance, in a family setting we may discuss boundaries, and in a workplace setting we may discuss productivity. Unless we are prepared to offer mental health resources to everyone present, as discussed in the next chapter, we do not approach the subject of mental health uninvited.

We know enough not to start a conversation about someone else's mental health, but what do we do when they mention it on their own? Let us start with productive, nonoffensive questions such as:

► **What do you mean when you say _____?**

Even if someone has disclosed a diagnostic label, such as depression, or if they mention a time when things were tough, that does not mean it is safe to assume you understand their story. Try genuinely asking someone what they mean by the terms they are sharing. That will give them an opportunity to see you are not acting on assumptions based just on the label but will show rather that you sincerely care to listen to them and understand them. In a climate where many people will try to brush past mental health conversations because such conversations can be anxiety-provoking and uncomfortable, this level of listening can mean a lot to people. If you are speaking in a professional context, it is possible that this question could be seen as an inappropriate, unnecessary inquiry into the nature and severity of a person's disability. Therefore, you may be better off skipping to the next question.

► **What do you want me to know when you say _____?**

This question is similar to the previous one, except now we are asking what the person specifically wants us to glean from what they are sharing instead of just clarifying what they mean. This is an important question because it recognizes that you have a limited, outside view of their situation rather than assuming that you understand it. Moreover, it lets the person know you want to follow their direction in forming your view, and it gives you a chance to hear what they want. In a professional setting, it also gives that person a chance to explain if they are asking for help of some kind, such as a reasonable accommodation.

► **What terms do you prefer I use?**

This question is all about ensuring that the language you use to discuss mental health is not offensive to the person you are talking with. It may be that they are unclear themselves about which terminologies they prefer, they may be unfamiliar with the idea that there are different terms, or they may be inconsistent in their preferences. All of that is okay. A large reason for asking this question is to remind the person that you are trying to follow their wishes. The sense that you are making this effort may make more of a positive impact than if you actually end up using the "correct" terms for the circumstance. Note that this is not an opportunity for you to share all that you have learned about terminologies, choices, and mental health experiences. After they have already shared the words they are using, it is simple to just say, "Is that the term you would like me to use?"

► **What role, if any, do you want me to play?**

We have discussed your role throughout this book, but until now we have approached it from your own perspective of what your role is. You have your own definition of what your place is in this person's life—be it friend, family member, colleague, or conflict resolution professional. But the person's definition may be very different. Never forget that your role is something you both define together, based on each of your boundaries. This question signals that you are ready to defer to them as to what role is a good fit for them. Note that you are not obligated to follow their wishes for the role you are going to play. You are still welcome to share your own boundaries and to clarify what your preferences and responsibilities are, using this question as a jumping-off point. All of this is especially important in professional contexts because often people may ask you to go beyond your professional boundaries and to be extra giving of your time, energy, or resources. They may ask you to side with them when you should remain impartial, and they may lean on you for emotional support when that is not your function. The simple way to deny these requests is to reiterate your role to the person and suggest that you will operate in the overlap between their wishes and what is possible for you.

► **Everything that happens is your choice. What do you want to do?**

Remember, our goal is always to empower the person we are speaking with. This question regarding what they want to do is a way to remind ourselves, and the person we are speaking with, that they are in the driver's seat. Be prepared for this question to occasionally elicit a sense of confusion or anxiety in the person you are speaking with—they may not like feeling that they have a choice, and they may believe that the system is such that their decisions are made for them. They of course have a right to that perspective, and it is a valid experience in a world where there is a shortage of mental health options available to people and where those options that are available have flaws. Whatever limits they perceive in the decisions that remain available to them, your job is to let them know that you understand that they make their own decisions, even if they are constrained in those decisions. You can reiterate that you are planning to help them make the most of the choices that are before them.

TAKEAWAY

Only ask about a person's mental health situation if they bring up the topic and limit your questions to what they decide to share. In these contexts, the best thing to do is to ask open-ended questions designed to let the person's choices dictate how you talk about mental health.

C. VALIDATE DIVERSE MENTAL HEALTH PERSPECTIVES

When we validate someone's perspective, we affirm their right to form their own beliefs and accept that they have shared their beliefs. You are agreeing that they are entitled to this belief, but you are not necessarily agreeing with the belief itself.

Validating perspectives is important because it helps the person feel heard, helps remind you that there are no "right" answers (only choices), and enhances your appreciation of their perspective.

The validation process can be divided into four steps in which you will learn to:

- Appreciate their point of view.
- Listen.
- Acknowledge their voice.
- Respect their choices.

TAKEAWAY

Validating someone's perspective helps them feel heard and empowered. It does not require that you agree with their point of view, but only that you respect it.

i. Appreciate Their Point of View

This book began with an overview of the diverse viewpoints people can have about mental health. Now is your chance to honor all of those viewpoints. Begin by reminding yourself, always, that everyone forms their own view of mental health. Now try to understand the person you are speaking with. You can use the worksheet below.

Remember not to assume anything: be earnest and open to hearing their view.

Appreciate Mental Health Perspectives Worksheet (Tool)

When you are trying to understand a person's perspective, consider the following questions. Remember not to assume anything because each person is different. Avoid asking someone about their experiences in invasive ways and do not make any inappropriate disability inquiries. You should consider these questions only if someone has decided to disclose these things to you about their mental health. You may never know the answers to all of these questions, but you can still use this worksheet as a tool to show you are sensitive to other perspectives.

What are their roles?   (e.g., peer, supporter, professional, all of the above)
What beliefs do they have about mental health?   (e.g., about causes of mental health problems, labels, treatments)
What experiences have they had that might influence their thinking?   (e.g., past symptoms, side effects, clinicians, services, cultural experiences, mental health communities)

ii. Listen

The next thing you have to do is listen. If you are a mediator, you likely already have extensive training in how to listen through a technique called reflective listening, which means repeating what the person said so that they have a chance to feel heard and to reflect on their thoughts. It is important to repeat back the important things that were said to demonstrate that you are listening and to give the person a chance to interact with their own ideas and make their own decisions. Entire books and courses focus on acquiring this skill, which seems simple but actually requires a lot of practice to get right. The following tool provides a general review primer on reflective listening skills.

Reflective Listening Tipsheet (Tool)

Reflective listening means repeating what was said, in the person's own words, without adding any extra framing, spin, advice, or input. It gives you the opportunity to validate their perspective, and, if others are nearby, it gives them a chance to hear the person's voice from a third party. It also allows them to correct you if you misheard them, or it may give them an opportunity to correct themselves.

Below are some tips for reflective listening:

Effective Listening

- Minimize distractions.
- Don't interrupt.
- Make eye contact.
- Look like you're listening.
- Be aware of your biases and try to manage them.

How to Reflect

- Repeat some or all of what the person just said, or paraphrase it.
- Try to use their own words.
- Say nothing extra from your own point of view.
- Wait for their response.

What to Reflect

- Reflect the feelings, facts, or thoughts that the person seemed to care about the most.

Potential Phrases to Help Your Begin Your Reflection

- So you feel _____.
- It sounds like you _____.
- You're saying _____.
- It seems that you _____.
- You're wondering _____.
- You're feeling _____.
- You're thinking _____.

iii. Acknowledge Their Voice

When we validate someone's perspective through engaging their point of view and reflective listening, we do not have to agree with that perspective. But we do have to respect that the person has a valid perspective rather than dismiss it entirely. This is especially important when we are discussing mental health needs because people are often dismissed when their perspectives are linked to mental health problems or emotions. Here are some simple things you can say to acknowledge someone's voice, depending on what your role may be:

- "Thank you for sharing your perspective on that. I am glad I had this opportunity to learn more about your feelings and experiences."

- "It is not my role to render an opinion in this conflict, but your voice matters a great deal."

- "I disagree with what you are saying but I am glad to have heard it and have gotten to know your point of view."

TAKEAWAY

After you listen, it is helpful to say something to let the person know that you value their voice regardless of whether you disagree with their beliefs.

iv. Personal Story: I Think You're Manic!

When I was first hospitalized and diagnosed with bipolar disorder, the medication I was taking required a blood level to see that it was working, so I regularly begged to get my blood drawn to see if it had increased enough to warrant my discharge. One day, the doctor was annoyed by my begging, so they asked me to hold out my arm and keep it still. I did so, and he said, "this means your level isn't high enough. If it was therapeutic, you would have tremors." Tremors are a possible side effect of the medicine I was taking.

This was a rude awakening that made me feel like I was being treated more as a clinical specimen than as a human being. I would later discover that I did not ever manifest that side effect, except during overdoses, so the doctor was technically wrong to check for the tremors as an indicator of my blood levels, in addition to having stigmatized me by reducing his normal clinical analysis to that side effect.

Yet this was not the most upsetting dismissal I experienced during my times in that hospital. I had befriended a nurse, Sam, who would sometimes talk with me during his shift. One day, when I was soon to be discharged, I started telling him about my future plans. I talked about studying for the LSAT and going to law school or working on a book about my experiences. After sharing these ideas, I asked Sam, "So, what do you think?"

Turning to me with a big smile, he said, "I think you're manic!" before walking off. Throughout my life I had been dismissed by people for a host of reasons: they occasionally thought I was rude or long-winded and the list goes on. But this moment changed my life. It was the first time some-one looked me in the eyes and decided that it did not matter what I had been saying because they were going to see me through the lens of my mental illness instead of treating my voice with respect. Never in my life had I felt as disempowered as I did in that first moment when Sam walked away chuckling.

But make no mistake: these dismissals happened all of the time and not just when I was in the hospital. For example, one psychiatrist told me he was not paying attention to what I said at face value; rather, he viewed my condition as an ongoing fire in my brain that needed to be man-aged. I asked him if he was listening to me or if he was trying to extinguish my current voice and bring out the me that he believed might be trapped behind those flames he was imagining. He said, "Interesting choice of words, extinguish" and left it there.

These clinical examples are only some of the many ways people can disconnect from what an-other person is saying and choose to focus on their mental illness instead. This is why it is so vitally important that we always make the effort to let people know that their voices matter and that they are being heard.

v. Respect Their Choices

Validation begins with appreciating the person's point of view and progresses to listening to them while also acknowledging their voice. The last step is to respect their choices. The easiest way to do this is to frame everything as a decision for them to make, rather than treating anyone's opinion or idea as a definitive answer. This book has shared many ways of thinking like that. Here are a few more questions you might ask yourself to help emphasize the person's decisions:

- What parts of this situation are in the person's control? What are their options in these as-pects?

- What are this person's rights? How can you help them feel empowered with these rights?

- Are there any ways people have treated this person like they did *not* have a choice? How can you help them see that they do?

By asking these questions, you can do some gut-checks and figure out where the decision points may lie in this conflict. Then all you have to do is ask open-ended questions about these decisions, al-ways emphasizing that the choices are up to the person you are speaking with.

TAKEAWAY

Pay attention to the different choices involved in the conflict and emphasize them.

D. SHARING CHALLENGING INFORMATION: DON'T NEGATE. ELABORATE!

A common question that arises in mental health situations revolves around how you can share challenging information without offending someone. Challenging information can include any content that presents a different or contradicting view, triggers a sensitivity, crosses a boundary, feels disempowering, is critical, or seems pessimistic. While this issue of sharing challenging information is quite ubiquitous, people ask me about it most often when they start to discuss the language of delusions and bizarre beliefs. In these situations, they often have a desire to correct a person's thoughts. The process of sharing challenging information is also applicable to virtually any life choice where a family member or anyone might wish there was a way to expand that person's views to also consider additional factors in their decisions.

Before you consider offering challenging information, it is helpful to reflect on your role. A family member or a supporter may have a trusting relationship in which it makes sense to share challenging information that a manager or conflict resolver might not share. Likewise, a conflict resolver or manager might consider sharing particular in-role challenging information tidbits as part of their professional responsibilities. This information can include policies, process limitations, deadlines, and other pieces of information that are appropriate within the context of their professional relationship.

Sharing challenging information is a delicate matter. Although this kind of sharing may seem wrong because we have been emphasizing the importance of following someone's lead, it is still possible to share challenging information without disempowering the person (though some hurt feelings and frustrations can still ensue when they are left facing information that challenges their perspective).

The first step for sharing challenging information is to follow the techniques we just explored about validating the person's perspective. Show an earnest interest in what they are saying and remember the lessons from this book so that you can manifest a sincerity in these efforts. Engage in reflective listening, taking extra care to confirm that you have accurately heard their point of view because you would like them to know that, throughout this entire process, you care about their point of view. Continue to validate anything new they share in this conversation.

Now that the stage has been set to have an initial rapport, it is helpful to frame this next step as a decision this person can make rather than you unilaterally forcing a conversation on them. As a preamble, you can cite other times this person already has made decisions; this will help them feel that they have a history of being in control of these discussions. Emphasize the choices they have now and validate any priorities they express related to these choices or anything else.

Then ask them for permission to share information about whatever decision you were hoping to add your perspective about. Remind them that you value their voice. Also remind them of your role in their life (from your perspective) and offer to share more information with them. If they say no, accept their choice. Remember: conflict resolution is about respecting peoples' autonomy, and so no means no. Also keep in mind that conflict resolution processes are not limited to single conversations; rather, you are building a relationship with this person. Accepting their "no" today and tomorrow and the next day can be seen as an investment in proving that you truly do value their autonomy rather than pretending that you do and then trying to force a conversation. Later on, they may approach you to follow-up once they have learned to trust that you are sincerely deferring to their choices.

Assuming they want to have the challenging information conversation, it is important to maintain an empowering tone throughout. That means working hard not to share any judgments about their decisions, the factors they believe are important, their understanding of things, or anything else. It also means exerting no pressure: it is important to maintain the attitude that everything is their decision throughout this conversation. Even if some external urgency exists, for some reason, your goal should still be to ensure that this conversation does not feel urgent.

Finally, avoid issuing any kind of ultimatum or command if you can help it. Even if a work policy has a firm limit or if a family boundary remains solid these boundaries are still something that could potentially be framed as this person's choice as much as possible, with the policy or boundary being treated as external information as opposed to a demand coming from you. You can frame the boundaries as choices by sharing them nonjudgmentally and then asking, "How do you want to handle this policy?" or "How do you want to address this rule of the house?"

When you are sharing challenging information, it can be helpful to conceptualize it as falling in the following categories:

- **Statistical Likelihoods**

  Sometimes you may want to share a likelihood based on data or experiences that show a specific trend. This may be citing a pattern of past incidents or a research study or any data that reflects a larger, global trend. When you do this, it is important to remember that it is inappropriate to generalize any trend to any individual. While the data might be meaningful for large populations, every single person has their unique experience, and so they are entitled to their full range of options. When you are talking about statistical likelihoods, you may say something like:

  "Every choice is always up to you. I know you want _____ and just want to share some information that _____ has tended not to work out well for people in the past, based on [research / your psychiatrist's experience / etc.]."

- **External Power Imbalances**

  An external power imbalance is a discussion about an outside force that is beyond anyone's control. That outside force may be company policy, the legal system, or anyone who has more power in the situation. It is important to remember that these power imbalances reflect real limits to someone's choices, but they also may not be just. They could very well be discriminatory, tinged with inappropriate prejudices and biases. Thus, it can be an extra sensitive matter to talk about these dynamics. Be ready to validate hurt feelings about this disempowerment, while also doing the best you can to outline the available choices. When you are talking about external power imbalances, you might say something like:

  "I know you want to leave the hospital. I also want to let you know that once people are in the hospital, there are rules that make it difficult to leave without the doctor agreeing."

- **Outside Perspectives**

  Outside perspectives are other points of view that this person may not appreciate. Recognizing other people's views is a challenge for anyone in any conflict, regardless of the presence of a mental health condition. These external views could be from other parties in the conflict or from people who are not involved. When you are talking about outside perspectives, you may say something like this:

"I respect that you do not feel like what happened when you were not feeling well was a big deal and you would rather not discuss it. Some of the other people who were there do still care about it and want to talk about it."

▶ **Personal Concerns**

Personal concerns will not likely arise in professional settings such as in a workplace or a conflict resolution practitioner's relationship with a party because they belie a sense of professionalism; all concerns can be framed in those professional power dynamics and outside perspectives instead. By contrast, a supporter with a personal relationship such as a trusted family member or a friend may find themselves in the position of sharing some of their personal concerns. They may do so by saying something like:

"Your perspective matters to me and I am glad that you shared how confident you feel about going to school across the country. I personally have some concerns because of stress that I experienced when problems occurred the last time you tried to do this."

TAKEAWAY

Avoid sharing challenging information without permission and be sure to take the time to have the conversation in a way that feels empowering to the person you are engaging.

i. Sharing Challenging Information Checklist (Tool)

Step 1: Validate What the Person Shared.

☐ Show an earnest interest in their perspective.

☐ Sincerely repeat back what they shared, ideally in their own words, to show that you are listening (ex. "So you feel _____").

☐ Ask them if you got it right (ex. "You value_____, is that right?").

☐ Ask them if there is anything else they would like to share.

☐ Validate anything new that they share.

Step 2: Frame the Conversation as a Decision.

☐ Highlight the areas where the person made a choice in the past.

☐ Emphasize the choices they have now.

☐ Validate any priorities they expressed.

Step 3: Ask if They Would Welcome Information about a Decision.

☐ Remind them that you value their voice.

☐ Remind them of your role.

☐ Offer to share more information.

Step 4: Share Challenging Information without Imposing Judgments, Pressure, or Commands.

☐ **Use statistical likelihoods.**
Ex. "Every choice is always up to you. I know you want _____ and just want to share some information that _____ has tended not to work out well for people in the past, based on [research / your psychiatrist's experience / etc]."

☐ **Explain external power imbalances.**
Ex. "I know you want to leave the hospital. I also want to let you know that once people are in the hospital there are rules that make it difficult to leave without the doctor agreeing."

☐ **Describe outside perspectives.**
Ex. "I respect that you do not feel like what happened when you were not feeling well was a big deal and you would rather not discuss it. Some of the other people who were there do still care about it and want to talk about it."

☐ **Share personal concerns.**
Ex. "Your perspective matters to me, and I am glad that you shared how confident you feel about going to school across the country. I personally have some concerns because of stress that I experienced when problems occurred the last time you tried to do this."

ii. Reflect on Your Role Worksheet (Tool)

When trying to understand your role, consider the following questions:

What is your job description?

Who do you serve?

What is the scope of your responsibilities?

Remember that your role determines what behavior is appropriate or not appropriate to comment on. Labeling people is not appropriate unless your role is to diagnose them as part of the services you provide.

You may have a professional responsibility to be responsive to someone's request for help due to their disability, but otherwise it is best to avoid making guesses about who may or may not have a disability and to refrain from unnecessary disability inquiries.

E. LISTEN TO THEIR NEEDS INSTEAD OF THEIR POSITIONS

One of our goals in conflict resolution when mental health needs are involved is to treat a person with mental health needs as we would treat anyone else. Much of what we have learned so far has been part of our efforts to mitigate bias by managing assumptions, emphasizing choices, and developing a cultural sensitivity to how we talk about mental health. But what about when there is actually a conflict to discuss? Should any special considerations be in play for the conflict conversation?

The short answer is no. In a standard conflict resolution process, we begin by having each party share their point of view and listen to one another. The next step is to start asking open-ended questions so that the conversation progresses from each participant's initial position to their underlying interests and needs. A position is a specific demand about an issue, while the underlying needs are the reasons why people care about those demands. There is not much to discuss if people remain stuck clinging to their positions. But if they shift the conversation to their needs, they can work together to brainstorm possible agreements.

This is what happens in any conflict, with or without the presence of a mental health problem. It is no different here. The following lists some common needs that arise when mental health situations are discussed. Note that they are universal needs that have nothing particular to do with mental illnesses. This is because we are all on the same spectrum.

Common Needs

- Respect
- Safety
- Autonomy
- Stability
- Inclusion
- Support
- Privacy
- Fairness
- Trust

In order to shift the conversation toward needs, you can try asking the following questions:

- Why do you want _____?"
- What would _____ do for you?"
- What do you mean by _____?
- "What are specific examples of _____?"

TAKEAWAY

Conflicts involving mental health needs involve positions and needs just like any other conflicts. Ask open-ended questions to shift from positions and surface underlying needs. This will set the stage for brainstorming possible agreements.

i. Positions and Needs Worksheet (Tool)

When you face a conflict, each person has **positions** (the things they want) and **needs or interests** (the reasons they want them)

Questions to Ask to Learn Needs

- "Why do you want _____?"
- "What would _____ do for you?"

Mapping Positions and Needs

	YOURS	THEIRS
POSITION		
Need #1		
Need #2		
Need #3		

Brainstorm

Please use the space below to brainstorm ways to meet both of your needs.

_____

_____

_____

F. REALITY-TEST AGREEMENTS

Once people begin brainstorming agreements, it is important that everyone involved in the conflict reality-test, or test the options being discussed. This is not meant in any way to question someone's sense of reality. Rather, this is a common conflict resolution practice and will likely be familiar to mediators. Reality-testing is meant to ensure that an agreement will actually work over time and will not break down.

Take, for example, a situation in which two people keep getting extremely upset with one another and are lashing out by yelling. Imagine they have now cooled off and have reached an agreement. "From now on we will promise to be nice to one another." That sounds very nice in theory, but it may not be rooted in the reality of each person's experiences, needs, and choices. That is why it is helpful to check that every agreement meets five important criteria:

- **Is it specific**—Exactly how will this be done?
- **Is it realistic**—Is it feasible?
- **Is it balanced**—Do both parties have benefits and responsibilities?
- **Is it sustainable**—Will it work over time?
- **Is it updatable**—Do we have a plan in place to make changes if it does not work?

In the case above, the agreement is not specific because "nice" is a vague word, and each person may have different definitions of it. The agreement is likely not realistic because these people seem to have a pattern of losing control and not being able to maintain their "nice" demeanor. This is a balanced agreement in that it is equal to both parties; yet again it is not sustainable for the same reason that it is not realistic. Perhaps they can be nice for a short while, but it seems likely they may have future clashes over time. Finally, there is no plan to update this agreement if it does not work out. That means that if there is another incident, both people may fight over the breached agreement instead of troubleshooting the problem.

When we develop our agreement, we want to ask open-ended questions regarding these five criteria to do a reality check and look for ways to correct these challenges. Through this exercise, the parties may get more specific about what "nice" looks like, and they may change their plan so that it is more realistic. Perhaps they will agree to apologize as soon as possible when they do not act "nice," rather than expecting each other to have perfect performance. These are just some examples of how testing the agreement collaboratively with open-ended questions across these dimensions can help improve it.

TAKEAWAY

Reality-test agreements in conflicts involving mental health needs as you would any other agreements.

i. Reality-Check Your Agreement Checklist (Tool)

When reaching any kind of agreement, remember to test that it will work going forward. Ask yourself:

☐ **Is it specific?**

Would a stranger looking at this agreement be able to figure out exactly what, how, and when it would be done? Be sure to clarify all of these details.

☐ **Is it realistic?**

Can this actually be done or is it wishful thinking? Has anyone had trouble following similar agreements in the past? How can we change this to make it possible or easy for us to do?

☐ **Is it balanced?**

Does everyone get some benefit from this agreement, and does everyone have comparable responsibilities under this agreement? Is it appealing to all involved? Be sure the agreement is not lopsided.

☐ **Is it sustainable?**

Is everyone able to do fulfill this agreement over time? Will something change in the future to make it harder to do? Plan ahead to make sure this agreement will last.

☐ **Is it updatable?**

Did you agree on a way to make changes in case this agreement does not work out as planned? This is an important issue so you can continue improving the agreement in the future rather than fight about technicalities.

G. SOME CHALLENGING CONVERSATIONS RELATED TO MENTAL HEALTH

Sometimes challenging topics may arise in conflicts related to mental health. It's important to remember that you can address these conflicts as you would any other conflict rather than see them as something different. That said, there are some helpful ideas to keep in mind when you are engaging in certain kinds of challenging conversations.

General Conflict Tips

- Remember that this is about understanding one another's ideas rather than critiquing them.

- Your goal is to use open-ended questions to learn about why the person has formed their position.

- Do **not** respond to a position with a counterposition or assess if it is a good idea.

Trauma Conversation Tips

- Recognize that anyone can have experienced trauma and use trauma-informed practices with everyone (be sensitive, empowering, and transparent).

- Do not ask about traumatic experiences but be supportive if the person brings it up.

Label Conversation Tips

- Recognizing labels may relate to disempowering or stressful past experiences.

- Listen reflectively to appreciate the labels and language each person prefers, and their feelings regarding different labels.

Sensitivities Conversation Tips

- Avoid criticizing someone for ways they are sensitive (e.g., don't say they are overreacting).

- Remember that treatment can be a sensitive subject; it is often a source of pain, stress, and trauma, but you never know who may see it that way and who may not

Lifestyle Choices Conversation Tips

- Try to appreciate why a person wants a certain lifestyle even if you do not feel it is realistic.

- Ask questions in support of their goals rather than emphasize criticisms or limitations.

> ## TAKEAWAY
>
> **Be ready to treat this conversation like any other, while also keeping in mind the lessons you learned to be sensitive to trauma, labels, sensitivities, and lifestyle choices.**

H. FAMILY COMMUNICATION PLANNING CONVERSATIONS

You might use some questions with families that are having mediations about how they communicate about mental health. The questions do not single out any one person's needs; rather, they keep everyone on an equal footing.

Below I list the communication questions. Like all other sections of this book, we would only have mental health conversations after someone else invited them; otherwise we would respect their privacy:

Terms We Use to Discuss Needs and Issues

- What does a mental health need look like for each family member?

- What language will we use in referencing mental health needs and issues?

- What other kinds of needs and issues would we like to discuss?

- What language would we like to attach to these issues?

Understanding Our Communication Needs and Goals

- What do we need to hear to feel safe and okay?

- What is easy for us to express?

- What is hard for us to express?

- How can we help each other communicate?

- What are each of our goals in talking with one another?

- What are positive aspects of our communication in the past? How can we encourage more of that positive communication?

- What are problems from our communication in the past? How can we avoid those problems?

How We Discuss Mental Health Problems

- When is it appropriate to discuss the problem?

- How often would we like to discuss the problem?

- What is the best way to start these conversations?

- How should we frame discussions if we believe a behavior is due to a mental health need?

- How will communication change with different levels of instability / concern about instability?

Sharing Information

- How do we want to share information about our needs with others?

- What are our plans for protecting privacy?

TAKEAWAY

There are a lot of different ways families may choose to discuss mental health. Remember to emphasize and discuss their choices rather than assuming you know what they want.

i. Family Sensitivity Conversations

A model has been developed that can be used to empower people living with mental health problems so that they can make choices about how they stay well, how they manage triggers, how they recognize warning signs, and how they take care of problems. This model is called the Wellness Recovery Action Plan (WRAP),[125] and it has been adapted for public use by the Substance Abuse and Mental Health Services Administration (SAMHSA).

As part of my mediation practice, I have adapted this personal plan for use in an agreement template that a family can use to discuss everyone's sensitivities. In order to keep these conversations balanced, it is vital to discuss everyone's needs equally rather than fixate on the person believed to have the most serious mental health needs.

Below are some questions that will help family members understand and address one another's sensitivities. The quotes presented with these questions are adapted from the SAMHSA Action Planning for Prevention and Recovery Guide.[126]

Note: Make sure to discuss all family members' triggers, warning signs, and needs and make plans for **everyone**—do not single anyone out. Remember not to have mental health conversations unless a party has asked to have that conversation. This will avoid unnecessary disability inquiries.

---

[125] Copeland, M. E. (2002). Wellness Recovery Action Plan: A system for monitoring, reducing and eliminating uncomfortable or dangerous physical symptoms and emotional feelings. *Occupational Therapy in Mental Health, 17*(3–4), 127–150.

[126] Substance Abuse and Mental Health Services Administration (2003). Action Planning for Prevention and Recovery. Retrieved from https://www.npaihb.org/wp-content/uploads/2018/12/action-planning-for-recovery.pdf

Triggers

"Triggers are external events or circumstances that may produce very uncomfortable feelings, such as anxiety, panic, discouragement, despair, or negative self-talk."

- What triggers affect our family?

- What things can we try to do to comfort ourselves and each other after triggers happen and so prevent reactions from becoming worse?

- How will we adjust this plan in the future?

Early Warning Signs

"Early warning signs are subtle signs of change that indicate you may need to take further action; they are internal processes that may or may not result from stressful situations."

- How have you felt in the past when things didn't feel quite right?

- What warning signs have we noticed in each other?

- What can we try to do to support ourselves and each other after signs occur and thereby prevent problems from becoming worse?

- How will we adjust this plan in the future?

When Things Are Breaking Down

"In spite of your best efforts, your problems may progress to the point where they are very uncomfortable, serious, and even dangerous."

- What things happen that make family members feel situations are getting significantly worse?

- How will we determine, individually, that things are breaking down?

- How will we determine, as a family, that things are breaking down?

- How will we adjust this plan in the future?

I. MENTAL HEALTH SENSITIVITY CHECKLIST (TOOL)

This checklist provides you with reminders and reflection questions to help you be sensitive to someone with mental health experiences. It is meant to be a quick tool to help you reflect on important aspects of being sensitive to anyone's potential mental health needs.

I acknowledge that . . .

- ☐ Mental health experiences often include struggles and confusion.
- ☐ Mental health choices are personal and there are no "right" answers.
- ☐ Mental health journeys are often long with no quick fixes.

Language

- ☐ Do you know what terms this person prefers to use to discuss mental health?
- ☐ Have you asked this person what they mean by the terms they are using?
- ☐ Are you using person-first language?

Identity

- ☐ Do you know this person's role(s) in the mental health system?
- ☐ Are you mindful that everyone experiences their identity uniquely, even if they are part of communities with shared perspectives?
- ☐ Are you careful not to make generalizations?

Choices

- ☐ Do you appreciate that this person has formed their own beliefs about causes, labels, and treatments in mental health?
- ☐ Do you appreciate this person's values?
- ☐ Have you validated this person's expressed beliefs?
- ☐ Have you empowered this person to make their own choices?
- ☐ Have you supported the mental health choices this person has made?

Experiences

- ☐ Are you mindful that two people with similar objective experiences may have different subjective reactions?
- ☐ Are you aware that this person may have had traumatic experiences?
- ☐ Are you accepting that this person may be sensitive in ways you do not understand?
- ☐ Are you sensitive to the challenges this person may face during transitions?

CHAPTER 8

DEVELOP UNIVERSAL, ACCESSIBLE PRACTICES

Throughout this book, we have emphasized that it is important not to assume any person needs help. Rather, we should have universal processes for offering help to everyone in the same way. The gold standard framework for doing so is called universal design.

> ### TAKEAWAY
> There are simple ways to offer help to everyone without singling out people with mental health conditions or other disabilities.

A. A UNIVERSAL DESIGN FRAMEWORK FOR ACCESSIBILITY

The term *universal design* was coined by Ronald Mace, and it was originally designed to promote accessibility in architecture.[127] The framework is so useful that it has been applied to many other contexts beyond the built environment. In the world of teaching, universal design methodologies are used to help teachers incorporate practices that appeal to a variety of different student learning styles. In the world of technology, different interfaces have been designed to be accessible to a wide variety of needs.

The idea behind universal design is that we can structure our world so that it is automatically flexible in accommodating the needs of people with diverse abilities. This way, these people can feel that they belong instead of needing to ask for special treatment. Not having to ask for special treatment is especially important when we are dealing with mental health needs, given the societal stigma that often discourages a person from disclosing a mental health condition.[128]

Universal design is special not just because people living with disabilities are protected from having to disclose, but also because everyone who accesses the structure or process can benefit from the enhanced design. A classic example is wider doorways, which make it possible for someone with a scooter to enter a building easily without assistance, while also making it easier for someone who does not have

---

[127] Story, M. F., Mueller, J. L., & Mace, R. L. (1998). *The universal design file: Designing for people of all ages and abilities.* North Carolina State University.

[128] Bos, A. E., Kanner, D., Muris, P., Janssen, B., & Mayer, B. (2009). Mental illness stigma and disclosure: Consequences of coming out of the closet. *Issues in Mental Health Nursing, 30*(8), 509–513.

a disability but is carrying groceries or moving furniture. As we discuss possible adjustments to our conflict resolution processes, you will see that they support everyone's mental health needs, not just those of people who have disabilities.

With regard to conflict resolution, I have developed a model that adapts universal design principles to help practitioners develop effective processes, adapt to client needs, and market their work in ways that make it appealing to diverse audiences of all kinds of abilities and backgrounds. It is rooted in seven key universal design principles, which were developed in 1997 by a working group at the North Carolina State University, led by Ron Mace.[129] These principles include equitable use, flexibility in use, simple and intuitive use, perceptible information, tolerance for error, low effort, and appropriate space.

i. Equitable Use

Equitable use means that the way the environment or process is designed is useful and marketable to people with different abilities. In the world of architecture, we want to make sure that whatever structure is being constructed is appealing to someone who may have different mobility needs.

In adapting this principle to conflict resolution, we want to make our conflict resolution process equally appealing to people of different backgrounds. Now of course among these people are those with different mental health needs, but we are not limited to people with psychiatric diagnoses. We can adjust our practices to all kinds of backgrounds.

For instance, there is one type of person who always prefers conflict resolution—someone who likes to talk and is comfortable articulating their point of view. Similarly, some people prefer avoiding conflict resolution because they are not comfortable talking through problems, and they also feel outmatched by others who are more assertive. These disparities occur across all races, genders, disability levels, and mental health conditions. Through all these communities there are talkers and avoiders. The principle of equitable use suggests that we must find a way to make our conflict resolution process appealing to both of them. Do you have any ideas about how you might do that?

ii. Flexibility in Use

Flexibility in use means that the design accommodates a wide range of individual preferences and abilities. In a building, it means that there may be multiple ways to enter and get around the place so that people with different abilities can choose the way that works best for them without having to ask anyone for special help. There may also be multiple ways to use a specific entrance, such as a combination ramp–stairs entryway.

In academic instruction, flexibility in use may mean there are different options for students to learn the material. For example, there may be a college course with lectures for the people who learn by hearing, recitations for the people who learn by doing, and reading assignments for those who learn by reading. Some courses may present these as options for the student to choose from, so they have great flexibility in how they learn the material by relying on what works best for their style.

---

[129] Story, M. F. (2001). The principles of universal design. In W. F. E. Preiser & K. H. Smith (Eds.), *Universal design handbook*. (2nd ed., pp. 4.3–4.9). McGraw Hill.

What about conflicts? What can we do to provide flexibility in use in conflicts? Well, we can consider different times to meet to resolve the conflict, different durations of our sessions, different topics to focus on, different styles of communication (perhaps someone feels better working things out through writing so that they have time to formulate their thoughts and digest the other person's thoughts). We may provide optional resources for having support through the conflict.

Flexibility of use means that we offer a buffet of options for people to pick what works best for them. We still have to think about what kinds of options might be appealing to people with different kinds of needs, but we do not ever have to guess who has what needs because the users of our process will be able to self-select to get what they need. Can you think of some ways you might be able to be flexible in working through your conflict?

iii. Simple and Intuitive Use

If a design has a simple and intuitive use, that means that it is easy to understand regardless of different levels of experience, knowledge, and ability. In a building, this may mean that there is an easy way to tell an entrance is an entrance or directions are clearly mapped out. In instruction, it may mean that material is communicated as simply as possible.

For conflict resolution, it means we make sure that the process we are using is straightforward and easy to understand. In other words, we try to keep it as simple as possible. For instance, we might take turns speaking and try to give one another equal time if we are trying to resolve things on our own as a family. At work, it could mean having clear, easy processes for resolving conflicts with coworkers or seeking additional support from a manager or human resources professional. With regard to professional conflict resolvers, we may try to make sure the entire process is as intuitive as it can be.

What are some ways that you believe your conflict resolution process might be complex, and how can you make it simpler? Remember, the goal is to develop a process that benefits everyone.

iv. Perceptible Information

Perceptible information means that the design communicates necessary information effectively to the user. By contrast with simple and intuitive use, which means it is easy to understand without instructions, this principle focuses on being able to access whatever information is being provided. This could mean increasing the legibility of information, presenting it in multiple modalities, or clearly differentiating essential information from larger writings with less important details.

In conflict resolution, this is a big principle because so many people are confused as to the meaning of mediation and the various styles mediators use.[130] We want to ensure that people involved in a conflict understand what is going on by being careful to share all of our practices clearly and up front. Otherwise, people may come into the conflict resolution process with the wrong expectations. They may even get embroiled in a stressful conflict, expecting the mediator to intervene and protect them, only to discover, too late, that this mediator believes in "following the heat."

---

[130] Charkoudian, L., Ritis, C. D., Buck, R., & Wilson, C. L. (2009). Mediation by any other name would smell as sweet—or would it? The struggle to define mediation and its various approaches. *Conflict Resolution Quarterly, 26*(3), 293–316.

What can you do to make sure the people involved in your conflict resolution process understand your role, your style, and your practices before the session begins?

v. Tolerance for Error

Tolerance for error is one of my favorite principles of universal design. It means that we are doing everything we can to minimize the consequences of any kind of accident or mishap. It also means removing hazardous aspects of the process, clearly warning people to help them avoid mistakes, and developing fail-safe practices to reduce the chance of problems.

The classic example I give for tolerance for error is the fear people have in conflict that if they say the wrong thing, it will be held against them. Or, I cite the nervousness that if they make a bad impression on their mediator, they will never be able to be empowered after that. Whether you are a professional conflict resolver or a layperson, it is important to realize the value in thinking about ways to reduce the impact of mistakes and missteps.

How can you arrange your process so that everyone is protected from making costly errors? How can you reassure participants that they will be okay if they made a mistake?

vi. Low Effort

Low effort is my other favorite principle. It means that the design can be accessed comfortably without people getting drained and exerting themselves to use it. That could mean minimizing physical effort or repetitive actions or weird physical positions that create a strain.

Regarding conflict resolution, what does high effort look like? I picture someone who is red in the face ranting about the other person, or another person who looks completely drained by what they are hearing, or a third person frantically scribbling notes in a fervor while the other person is talking. Don't these sound like high effort situations?

Again, whether you are a professional conflict resolver or a layperson, it is great to think about ways you can reduce this strain when you are resolving conflicts. Can you think of any?

vii. Appropriate Space

With physical issues, appropriate space may mean being able to reach and access things regardless of body type and ability differences. How about the role of appropriate space in conflict resolution?

With regard to in-person sessions, appropriate space may mean how the room is structured so that everyone feels comfortable. With regard to virtual sessions, it is a similar idea, but different in the way the online process is structured. Can you think of any ways to ensure that your conflict resolution process has an appropriate space?

> ## TAKEAWAY
>
> **The seven principles of universal design are a helpful tool for thinking of ways to design your conflict resolution process to meet everyone's mental health needs, rather than waiting for someone to ask for help. That is especially important so that people with mental health needs do not have to disclose them and thereby can avoid experiencing feelings of stigma.**

B. SAMPLE ACCESSIBLE OPENING STATEMENT FOR MEDIATORS

The sample mediation opening statement presented below provides guidelines that can be included in any dispute resolution process. It shows how I have used some of the principles from the previous section in my own practice. See if you can tell which guidelines are linked to which principle.

Introduction and Explanation of the Process, Impartiality, and Confidentiality

Welcome to the mediation. A mediation is a conversation between the two of you. I provide no input. I make no decisions. My only role is to listen to each of you, reflect what you say, and provide support working through a process that can end in an agreement if that's what you choose. This process is confidential, and I am impartial, meaning I will not take sides. I have no bias or stake in the outcome. If you ever feel that is not the case, please say something.

Emphasis on Self-Determination

Being here is voluntary, and whatever happens is always your choice. We are here because you both wanted to be here to have a conversation and maybe reach an agreement.

Suggesting Guidelines

My job is to make this process as comfortable as possible for both of you so that you will want to be here. I'm going to suggest some guidelines, and it is up to you both if you would like to use them for our session:

1. **Minimizing stress.** If you agree, we will try to make this conversation as low-stress as possible. It means letting everyone know if you feel that things are getting too stressful, so we can decide together if we need to take a break or just check in.

2. **Allowing for mistakes.** If you agree, we will try to reduce the pressure of the conversation to "say the right thing at the right time." We'll have this conversation acknowledging that people may misspeak and giving everyone the opportunity to correct themselves later.

If one or more parties have asked for help with communication needs during a pre-session, I may suggest the following additional guidelines:

3. **Staying focused.** Sometimes in mediation, people can get into a lot of different topics when the parties have really only agreed to discuss one or two. Today, you have agreed to discuss [TOPIC 1] and [TOPIC 2]. If you like, I can note when we are expanding to other topics to help us stay focused on these topics.

4. **Taking breaks.** Because it can be uncomfortable to talk for long lengths of time, it might be a good idea for us to take a 5-minute break every 30 minutes.

5. **Communicating in other ways.** People often prefer to communicate in different ways. If anyone prefers, we can use written statements or other methods of communication during the session.

Did you notice which principles were linked to which provision? "Minimizing stress" is low effort, "Allowing for mistakes" is tolerance for error, and the other three are all flexibility in use.

Sharing these guidelines gives perceptible information about how I practice, and the language is written as simply as possible so that there is intuitive use as well as perceptible information.

The "Communicating in other ways" provision is also an example of equitable use, appealing to parties with varying preferences regarding communication styles instead of structuring the session using my communication preferences.

TAKEAWAY

It can be relatively straightforward to incorporate universal design principles into your conflict resolution practices.

C. WORKPLACE CASE STUDY: WORKPLACE HEALTH PROMOTION

Many workplaces would like to offer mental health services and referrals to their employees. They may invest in benefits like EAPs, health insurance, wellness staff, and pro-health programming to support employee well-being. It is important that any referrals to this programming be done in a universal manner that does not ever single out individual people who staff may suspect could benefit from the resources. Companies might do this effectively in several ways:

1. Openly promote these resources to everyone on a regular basis. This allows people to know about them without singling out any individual's behavior.

2. Create resource handouts that outline all of these resources in writing, and in these handouts include all of your resources—not just mental health resources—so that way the mental health resources are less stigmatized by not having them set apart.

3. If you feel the need to make referrals to resources, give out the handouts with all of the resources (mental health and nonmental health alike) and do so only in response to preexisting, objective

policies about when these resources will be distributed. For instance, any time someone has a certain number of absences in a month, then you give them this broad resource handout. This is an acceptable way to give a direct referral, as it is rooted in workplace behavior criteria rather than your subjective judgment and it is done without being linked to a question about a particular employee's mental health. Yet I would still advise being careful before doing this because people could still get offended.

TAKEAWAY

Do not single people out with referrals to your health and wellness services. If you want to share resources, make general promotion efforts using consistent, universal criteria.

D. ACCESSIBILITY SCENARIOS

For each of the seven accessibility principles, write how you might apply it in your conflict resolution process.

1. **EQUITABLE USE**

   How do you ensure the process is appealing and usable for all participants? And that it avoids segregating or stigmatizing the user?

2. **FLEXIBILITY IN USE**

   How do you ensure that the process accommodates a wide range of individual preferences and abilities?

3. **SIMPLE AND INTUITIVE IN USE**

   How do you ensure that the process is easy to understand regardless of the user's experience, knowledge, language skills, concentration level, or other factors?

4. **PERCEPTIBLE INFORMATION**

   How do you ensure that the process is communicating necessary information effectively regardless of ambient conditions or of the user's abilities?

5. **TOLERANCE FOR ERROR**

   How do you ensure that the process minimizes the hazards and consequences of accidental or unintended actions?

6. **LOW EFFORT**

   How do you ensure that the process doesn't require too much exertion for the parties (e.g., intense amounts of effort to maintain composure)?

7. **APPROPRIATE SPACE**

   How do you ensure that the process is conducted in a comfortable environment?

CHAPTER 9

PLAN FOR CHALLENGING BEHAVIORS

In chapter 6, we debunked the myth that mental health problems should be connected to our concerns about challenging behaviors, and in chapter 3, we learned how this linkage was actually the product of stigma and scapegoating. This chapter will present a framework for addressing challenging behaviors using impartial plans based on objective behavioral criteria that have nothing to do with mental health diagnoses or suspicions. In order to overcome stigmatizing attitudes about mental illness and challenging behaviors, it helps to put extra effort into making plans that can guide us in responding to challenging behaviors in an impartial manner.

A. STUDYING CHALLENGING BEHAVIORS IN CONFLICTS

Recognizing the need for advancement in how conflict resolvers address challenging behaviors in mediation, my company, MH Mediate, partnered with Justin Corbett of Advancing Dispute Resolution to launch the Survey on Participant Behaviors in Mediation. This 2013 research project was envisioned as a starting point for developing MH Mediate's interventions to help practitioners and others address challenging behaviors. Several years later, Rachel Canella was instrumental in summarizing the findings of the literature review and supporting further analysis of the study data.

As a precursor to the survey, we oversaw a literature review of over 40 publications published between 1985 and 2013 that identified challenging behaviors that practitioners were experiencing in mediation. Some of the behaviors identified from this review are included in the following list, with the caveat that disempowering framings are not my wordings but rather they were quoted directly from third-party viewpoints:

- A lack of trust
- Angry/Excess anger
- Being unable to schedule meetings
- Blaming orientations
- Blaming other party
- Calling the intake person three to five times a day
- Communicating condescension
- Compulsive
- Consistent behavior so inappropriate as to be more than merely disruptive
- Consistent misinterpretation of the intention
- Consistently failing to follow through during the scheduling process
- Counter-arguments
- Crying
- Delaying tactics

- Desire to "wound" other party member
- Displays nervous mannerisms
- Disputants not making previously agreed-to phone calls
- Disrespect from one party towards the other
- Distrust
- Domestic violence
- Dropping books
- Emotional outburst
- Engaging in social behavior that is grossly inept or inappropriate
- Erratic or unpredictable turns in conversation, demeanor, or behavior
- Exhibiting phobias that do not respond to repeated reassurances or reflective listening
- Expressing unrealistic goals
- Faces the wall
- Gives more value to their own actions
- Giving clipped responses
- Having self-righteous attitudes
- Hostile atmosphere arises
- Hostile non-verbal expression
- Insisting other party admit they are wrong
- Interpretations based on prejudicial beliefs
- Interrupting
- Keeps silent
- Lack of trust in information
- Laugh at spouse's questions
- Looking at the floor
- Lying
- Making moral judgments
- Making threats/demands of other party
- Minimizing/ ignoring others feelings
- Name-Calling
- Need to make others experience the negative emotions they feel
- Negative labeling
- No commitment to resolve conflict by the parties
- Nonassertive
- Ongoing challenges to mediator actions or suggestions
- Party does not fully understand the mediation process
- Party lacks the ability to identify his or her interests and to weigh the consequences of an agreement
- Pay too much attention to details
- Persistent reneging on decisions painstakingly arrived at during the same session
- Prejudice attitudes
- Provide contradictory instructions
- Putting forth settlement objectives impossible to achieve
- Questioning other party's honesty
- Refusing to respond
- Refusing to shake hands
- Repeats details or is a perfectionist
- Sarcasm
- Saying something offensive
- Self-centered
- Severe mood swings
- Severe withdrawal from the process
- Sexual castigation
- Shaking of head
- Shouting
- Showing up for meetings or sessions on the wrong days

- Substantial behavioral changes within the mediation process
- The continued and blatant inability to adhere to simple ground rules
- The repeated failure to focus on an agreed-upon topic
- Threatening to leave room
- Threatens withhold finances

- Throwing theatrical tantrums
- Understating needs
- Voices denials
- Whitewashing future effects
- Withdrawal
- Withholds responses
- Workplace bullying

These behaviors helped us develop categories to explore in our survey. The categories were also influenced by qualitative surveys of the NYC-DR Listserv operated by the City University of New York's Dispute Resolution Center and the National Association for Community Mediation (NAFCM) Listserv focused on community mediators. The surveyed behaviors included:

- Physical aggressiveness without contact
- Physical aggressiveness with contact
- Verbal aggressiveness
- Belittling, dismissive, or sarcastic language
- Continued conflict expansion and/or escalation
- Incomprehensible reasoning process
- Inability to weigh options
- Difficulty understanding the mediation process
- Inconsistent statements
- Onset of an acute physical incapacity
- Onset of an acute emotional/psychological incapacity
- Withdrawal from active participation
- Discomfort with the pace of the conversation

We reached out to over 2,000 mediators across the United States and recorded responses from 300 practitioners from all different types and levels of expertise (effectively representing the general population of mediators). Topics that the survey covered included mediator's confidence in identifying and dealing with challenging behaviors, procedures they had established to deal with these behaviors, their desires for clearer policies, and the prevalence of behaviors they encountered.

The participants' ages ranged between 19 and 69, with the majority of the sample coming from 60– to 69-year-olds (41.8%) or 50- to 59-year-olds (30.3%). In addition, 58.8% of the sample was female while 40.4% was male, and 44% of the sample were attorneys. From this survey, we found the following prevalence rates for the different categories of behavior. This was framed in terms of what percentage of the surveyed mediators had experienced these behaviors at least once in their career:

- Belittling, dismissive, or sarcastic language (97%)

- Inconsistent statements (95%)

- Verbal aggressiveness (94%)

- Conflict expansion or escalation (93%)

- Inability to weigh options (91%)

- Discomfort with the pace of mediation (88%)

- Incomprehensible reasoning (88%)

- Withdrawal from active participation (85%)

- Difficulty understanding the process (80%)

- Onset of acute emotional incapacity (61%)

- Physical aggressiveness without contact (56%)

- Onset of acute physical incapacity (20%)

- Physical aggressiveness with contact (10%)

We also learned that, despite the fact that over 85% of the mediators were acting on a case-by-case basis and over 60% expressed interest in clearer policies, they were still overconfident. Over 78% of mediators felt their abilities were above average, while only 1% believed they were below it. The fact that such a high percentage of those surveyed indicated they believed they were above average and only 1% said they fell below it is a sign of overconfidence consistent with findings from the literature on illusory superiority, a cognitive bias whereby people tend to overestimate their abilities relative to others.[131] In other words, though mediators showed a desire for plans, they also revealed some overconfidence about their own abilities, which may help explain the high percentage of practitioners choosing to operate on a case-by-case basis.

TAKEAWAY

Challenging behaviors are common. When surveyed, conflict resolvers have indicated they want better plans for addressing them.

B. WHY PLAN FOR CHALLENGING BEHAVIORS

There are five primary reasons to plan for challenging behaviors. The first reason is for the comfort of the practitioner. Anyone who has experienced a challenging behavior is familiar with the confusion and hesitation involved in responding. A clear plan allows a practitioner to feel comfortable and ready to respond to problems.

---

[131] Alicke, M. D., & Govorun, O. (2005). The better-than-average effect. *The self in social judgment, 1,* 85–106. Psychology Press.

Next, a plan allows a conflict resolver to be transparent. Have you ever had someone ask you why you chose to do something, and you were unable to answer? It is terrible to have that level of unpreparedness when responding to someone questioning whether you were fair in intervening in their challenging behavior. Having clear criteria and policies gives you the ability to explain why you did what you did.

Safety is a paramount concern in managing challenging behaviors. While this book does not give you any specific one-size-fits-all safety protocols, whatever approach you take to safety will be enhanced if you are acting on a robust plan rather than your own intuition.

Impartiality is perhaps the most important reason to create a behavior plan using objective criteria. Our goal in conflict resolution should always be to provide a fair, nonbiased experience. The best way to get close to that goal is by constraining our decision making and deferring to a set of behavior criteria that existed before we met the person in question.

The final reason for planning for challenging behaviors is to correct our own fallibility. We are just people, with good days and bad, and it is possible we may make mistakes. In *The Checklist Manifesto*, Atul Gawande writes about how checklists helped hospital staff avoid mistakes in the operating room (OR). In a survey of over 250 staff based on three months of using a checklist, 78% had observed the checklist preventing an error in the OR.[132]

TAKEAWAY

Planning for challenging behaviors allows us to feel comfortable, be transparent, maximize safety, be fair, and correct our own fallibility.

C. MOVING FROM "DIFFICULT PEOPLE" TO CHALLENGING BEHAVIORS

Just as it is wrong to profile people based on mental health labels, it is similarly inappropriate to label people based on their behaviors. It is important to put a wall up between people and their behaviors so that we do not link the two (Figure 9.1).

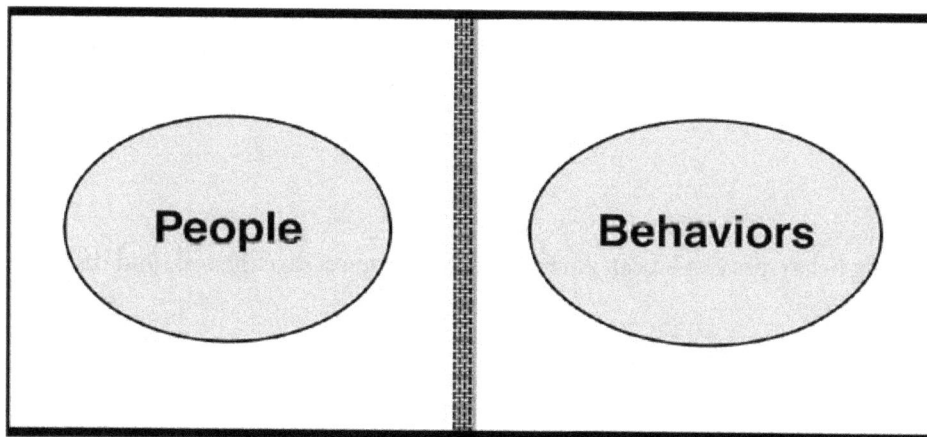

---

[132] Gawande, Atul. 2011. *The checklist manifesto*. Profile Books.

When we steer clear of terms such as difficult people, it allows us to prevent confusion because it compels us to specify the actual behavior that is causing a problem. It also helps us to remember our role by prompting us to reflect on why this behavior is relevant, instead of simply dismissing the person entirely. Finally, it helps us to avoid inadvertent discrimination. It is wrong to single someone out for different treatment based on our seeing them differently as a person, particularly if we are perceiving that this "difficult person" label is linked to the idea that this person has psychiatric symptoms.

TAKEAWAY

It is stigmatizing and nonproductive to use offensive labels such as "difficult people" instead of addressing challenging behaviors.

D. A FRAMEWORK FOR RESPONDING TO CHALLENGING BEHAVIORS

In order to respond effectively to challenging behaviors, it is important to create clear behavior thresholds that are objective and prepared before encountering the parties. This is in contrast to many peoples' practices of improvising based on their gut feelings.

i. Identify the Type of Behavior

Challenging behaviors can be divided into three key categories: emergencies, disruptions, and disconnects.

Emergencies include any kind of crisis that requires immediate attention and may necessitate reaching out to other professionals for support, including police, emergency medical technicians, and doctors. Anything extreme happening that demands the suspension of normal operating procedure is an emergency.

Disruptions are problems that impair the conflict resolution process, but do not rise to the level of an emergency. You may decide to deal with them right away, but it is not a definite, urgent necessity that you do so.

Disconnects are situations where you are not able to effectively communicate with one another; this communication gap means that the process has to change or be ended.

TAKEAWAY

Challenging behaviors can be categorized as emergencies, disruptions, and disconnects.

ii. Get Specific

In order to address a challenging behavior, we have to be specific about what makes it a problem. To do that, we have to clearly identify the problem behavior. Many things may bother us about a person. We therefore have to pinpoint which of their behaviors actually is a problem in the context of our role. Then we have to describe it in objective terms. Do not use any innuendo or judgment: be detached and plain-spoken about what is going on.

Finally, we have to be sure to remove any backstory we have attached to this situation. That means we do not label the person as difficult or start suspecting a mental health problem or ascribe any kind of intention to them. All we are doing is describing their behavior.

There are a lot of words besides "difficult" that are counterproductive because they do not tell us what the behavior actually is. Here are some examples:

- Aggressive
- Delusional
- Angry
- Frantic
- Erratic
- Irate

With all of these terms, we would need to ask more questions to find out what was going on. For instance, do we know what the word "aggressive" actually means? When I give workshops about getting specific, and someone mentions dealing with an aggressive party, I ask the audience if they have an idea what that is like and usually most people nod. Then I explain I have no idea what this person means. There is no way to know whether the person raised their voice, hit a table, used language that sounded threatening, or did something else—almost anything could be seen as aggressive, after all. I ask the participant what they meant, and it is always the case that everyone else had a different picture. Once, someone had used the word "aggressive" as their proxy from having had someone spit at their face. There is no way to really know what anyone is talking about unless we get past these generalizations and use specific language to discuss specific behaviors.

Getting specific also means pinpointing which behavior is the problem. Here is an example from a librarian that shows the challenges of being specific about challenging behaviors:

A frequent patron is an older man who is very loud, even if asked to lower his voice. Every time he enters the building, he announces he is a Vietnam Vet and expects special treatment because of that. He verbally abuses women on the staff and anyone who says anything to him at all. He seems to have no filter for what he says (profanity and abuse) and cannot control the volume of his voice. He disrupts everyone when he enters the building. The security guard has tried and failed to control his behavior, and usually asks him to leave the building, but that is not really addressing the situation.

Can you clearly identify what the challenging behavior is that we might respond to in that situation? Here are some possibilities, each of which would require its own criteria:

- Is very loud
- Does not follow direction (to lower his voice, "tried and failed to control")
- Expects special treatment
- Verbally abuses (we need to ask if this is a content issue, a volume issue, etc.)
- Targets women (is this some kind of discrimination)
- Uses profanity
- Commits abuse (we would need to ask what this is)
- Disrupts everyone (we would need to ask how)

When I give workshops, we often get vignettes like this from participants looking for assistance with a challenging behavior example they have encountered. The participants themselves are unclear which specific behaviors were the main problem because they had just been thinking of their experience as a single story of a "difficult person." As a group, we all have to work together to figure out which behavior from this list is the main one that the person is upset about and needs to consider intervening in. Often some behaviors are simply nuisances that are meant to be ignored based on the organization's policies, but that single story lumped them in with serious offenses that merit substantial interventions. Identifying behavior-based criteria and interventions in advance helps us to disentangle these complex narratives and focus on the truly challenging behaviors.

By the way, did you notice the backstory in that vignette that we need to ignore?

- Seems to have no filter
- Cannot control the volume of his voice

Both of these items are the librarian's personal hunches and part of their imagined narrative about why this person is doing what they are doing. They are the kinds of assumed capacity deficits that often lead someone down a path of stereotyping to guess that a mental health problem might be present as well. And they are entirely counterproductive to actually addressing the challenging behavior.

It is essential that we focus solely on objective observations without bundling them with our ideas of the person's intent or any other backstories, such as this librarian's assessment that the person has some kind of filter deficit.

TAKEAWAY

Select which specific behavior is a problem and then describe it in objective terms without adding in your idea of any backstory.

iii. Behavior Without Backstory Checklist (Tool)

Step 1: Pinpoint the Specific Behavior That Is a Problem.

- ☐ Ask yourself what this person is doing that you believe is inappropriate.
- ☐ Describe these behaviors in objective, unemotional language.
- ☐ If there are many instances of different challenging behaviors happening at once, look at them one at a time.
- ☐ Identify which of the behaviors is the biggest problem.
- ☐ Identify the policy or norm that is being violated and making it a problem.

Step 2: Evaluate That Behavior Based on Universal Criteria.

- ☐ Reflect on your normal values and policies.
- ☐ Ask yourself what the general criteria are for when this kind of behavior is a problem.
- ☐ Ask yourself what the typical response is for when this kind of behavior is a problem.

Step 3: Ignore Whatever Backstory You're Imagining.

- ☐ Accept that you may form ideas and labels as to who this person is due to conscious and implicit bias.
- ☐ Remind yourself that it is not helpful to profile a person and make guesses about their backstory to explain the behavior.
- ☐ Remind yourself that incorporating a backstory into your intervention may seem biased and may be counterproductive to addressing the behavior.

Step 4: Follow Your Plan for Addressing the Behavior without Profiling the Person.

- ☐ Follow your normal plan for responding to the challenging behavior, based on universal criteria.
- ☐ If you don't have a plan, do your best to make one based on the broader category of behavior instead of inventing one just for this one particular person or instance.

iv. Identify a Prompt to Act and the Intervention

For each behavior prompt you plan to act on, you can use the following template to help you prepare your behavior intervention:

Prompt	Action Steps

There are many training programs that teach different techniques in responding to behaviors. This framework does not make any decisions about which of these interventions are right. Rather, this tool ensures that whatever intervention you choose is evenly applied. That is to say, you will always perform the same intervention regardless of whether you are dealing with people of different races, abilities, genders, or other identity characteristics. To accomplish that impartial way of intervening, you can use this planning framework instead of relying on your gut feelings.

The most important thing to reflect on is your prompt for taking action. What is going to be your cue? The simplest cues are the mere presence of the behavior at all. For instance, it is easier for me to say I will give a warning whenever anyone yells instead of trying to come up with a more complicated scheme of assessing the volume, frequency, or impact of the yelling.

The best prompts are clear, principled, specific, and concise. You can review potential interventions from the Behavior Intervention Strategy Sheet that follows this discussion.

How do you decide how to make your prompt? Refer to the ethics inherent in your role, any policies at your organization, and any boundaries you have formed—typically in that order with ethics as the top priority followed by company policy and then filling in any gaps using your personal boundaries. Your boundaries will be different from those of other people, and that is okay. The goal of this planning exercise is not to achieve uniformity with everyone else, but rather to achieve internal consistency to reduce the chance that you will act in a biased manner.

TAKEAWAY

Plan ahead for challenging behaviors by identifying your prompt for action as well as the intervention you will use. The key is to use this plan instead of relying on your gut feelings.

v. Behavior Intervention Strategy Sheet (Tool)

Reminder: Be mindful of your organization's policies, your professional norms, and your personal boundaries when deciding an intervention.

Prevention

Are there ways that you can structure the environment or process to make the behavior less likely? Are there early phases of this behavior where you can intervene to prevent escalation?

- **Best Practice:** Use up-front guidelines to set norms for appropriate conduct. These can be administered on intake, through sharing written policies, through opening statements, and when interventions take place.

- **Caution:** Relying on your gut feeling instead of objective behavioral criteria may lead you to be biased in issuing warnings or process adjustments.

De-escalation

What can be done to de-escalate this behavior?

- **Best Practice:** Reminders about conduct guidelines, session purpose, and referral resources are options to de-escalate, as are debriefs of the behavior and session breaks.

- **Caution:** Be prepared for parties to feel singled out and challenge your fairness when you de-escalate.

- **Caution:** Always follow your personal practices, organizational practices, and session norms when deciding what behaviors to tolerate.

Emergency Response or Session Termination

When might this behavior become an emergency, or be related to an emergency? What emergency response will you take?

- **Best Practice:** Develop clear protocols for different emergencies—fire, acute incapacity, violence. Rely on behavioral criteria to prompt action, and do not hesitate to implement your plan.

- **Caution:** These practices should ideally be driven by your organization and experts in your field.

No Response

When might the behavior warrant no response?

- **Best Practice:** Decide in advance when you will not respond, using behavioral criteria.

- **Caution:** Not responding or overlooking behaviors with some parties but not others is a common source of biased interventions.

- **Caution:** Not responding to a challenging behavior can set lax expectations and make it harder to prevent later on.

vi. *Implementing Your Behavior Principles Checklist (Tool)*

This checklist provides you with reflection questions to help you plan how you will develop and share your personal behavior principles.

Adjusting Your Personal Practices

- ☐ Do I regularly remind myself of my plan?
- ☐ Do I refer to my plan when taking action?
- ☐ Are my boundaries consistent across different parties and situations?
- ☐ Am I taking consistent action when I do choose to act?
- ☐ Do I feel the need to plan for other behaviors?

Communicating Your Principles

What do you choose to share?

- ☐ The values or purpose behind your behavior practices
- ☐ Your efforts developing the practices
- ☐ Your actual guidelines

How do you choose to share your principles?

- ☐ Up-front guidelines
- ☐ Intake paperwork
- ☐ Consent for service
- ☐ Upon intervening
- ☐ When asked about policies
- ☐ When asked reasons for intervening
- ☐ Never

How do you share your practices, if you choose to share them?

- ☐ In writing
- ☐ Verbally
- ☐ Both
- ☐ I do not share them

Collaborating with Colleagues

- ☐ Did you explore the similarities and differences in your thresholds for intervening?
- ☐ Did you explore the similarities and differences in your interventions?

How do you reach consensus on administering your interventions?

- ☐ Follow the most liberal practice
- ☐ Follow the most conservative practice
- ☐ Reach an ad hoc agreement
- ☐ Do not reach consensus

Seeking Feedback

- ☐ Do you ask for feedback when the intervention happens?
- ☐ Do you ask for feedback in follow-up?
- ☐ Are you generally open for feedback?

Reflective Practice

- ☐ Do you engage in personal debriefs after each session?
- ☐ Do you participate in a reflective practice group?
- ☐ Do you receive supervision (professional or informal)?
- ☐ Do you receive informal feedback?
- ☐ Do you stay informed of your organizational practices and professional norms?

vii. Sample Guidelines for Preventing and De-escalating Disruptions (Tool)

The example below was created for use by libraries. The principles can be adapted to many different contexts.

Fairness (We Treat Everyone the Same)

- Staff are trained to be impartial and consistent, so all patrons have equal access and opportunities.
- We welcome feedback about your experiences and ways to improve our services so that they are fair.

Empowerment (We Empower Choices)

- We understand different people use library resources differently, and we want to present options.
- Whenever possible, we highlight choices available to patrons accessing services and resources.

Community (We Care about Everyone's Well-being)

- We care about creating a positive environment for the whole community.
- We are inclusive and welcoming to all patrons.

Responsibility (We Have Clear Boundaries)

- We all are responsible for our own behavior.
- We share clear expectations and boundaries for conduct.

Sharing (We Manage Shared Resources)

- We ensure people take good care of communal property and resources.
- We facilitate the fair distribution of shared resources.

viii. Talking Points for Disconnects (Tool)

Instead of blaming the other person for misunderstandings, try to stay neutral. Say things like:

"I'm having trouble understanding you."

> Instead of accusing them of having some kind of deficit or shortcoming, take responsibility for the disconnect yourself by framing it as a challenge you're experiencing.

"The steps I'm taking are what I do whenever I have trouble understanding a client or coworker."

> Do not do anything that makes them feel they are being singled out. Instead, remind them of the broader universal context. Explain that this is what you do when you are dealing with any disconnects.

"Do you have any ideas of how we can better understand each other?"

> Encourage them to help you figure out a way to connect.

"It's okay if we cannot understand each other; that happens sometimes."

> Do not put pressure on them or yourself to connect because sometimes disconnects cannot be repaired. Instead acknowledge that this challenge is happening but let them know it is not that unusual or bad. Taking this tone is important even if you are not sure they understand you.

E. CHALLENGING BEHAVIOR SCENARIOS

Here are some example situations you can plan for:

Emergencies

What are your personal principles and procedures for addressing the following potential emergencies?

- Medical emergencies
- Inclement weather
- Mental health emergency
- Violence
- Domestic violence
- Child endangerment

Include what criteria you use to determine if the incident has risen to the level of an emergency to trigger your personal principles.

Disruptions

What are your personal principles and procedures for addressing the following potential disruptions?

- Tangents
- Monopolization of time
- Distractions
- Lack of engagement

Include the criteria you use to determine if the incident has risen to the level of a disruption to trigger your personal principles.

Disconnects

What are your personal principles and procedures for addressing the following disconnects?

- Inability to understand one another
- Agreement to every option, even those that conflict with one another
- Third-party dominance
- Language barrier

Include the criteria you use to determine if the incident has risen to the level of a disconnect to trigger your personal principles.

Conclusion: We All Have Bad Days

Mental health needs are universal. We all have feelings, and we all have bad days. Often those bad days will happen when we are experiencing conflict.

Not everyone will be diagnosed with a mental health problem, but we all experience problems related to our mental health. Everyone knows what it is like to feel sad, worried, or overwhelmed. We also know these kinds of stressors will often occur during conflicts. That is why it is important that families, workplaces, and professional conflict resolvers learn how to effectively support people who may be experiencing challenges.

Anyone we meet may be experiencing difficulties. And so we must enter every conflict aware that mental health needs may be at play and that people may need support so that they can feel better as they work through these issues. At the same time, while we are being sensitive to everyone we encounter, we must also remember not to single anyone out. In this volume, we have covered techniques that can help anyone feel more empowered during conflicts. It is vitally important that we offer these techniques to everyone equally.

Remember, everyone's bad days and mental health problems manifest in different ways. It is not our role to diagnose. Rather, our role is to listen, validate their perspective, and support them in making their own choices through conflicts. If we ever shift into labeling, giving advice, or recommending treatment, then this becomes a different process entirely. It is no longer conflict resolution because it is biased toward guiding the person to our idea of what is helpful instead of honoring their self-determination.

The path to empowerment requires that we respect the other person is in the driver's seat of their own life choices. We must strive to listen to them without an agenda. Changing our responses based on our own ideas of what is best for the person is not just inadvertently paternalistic; it can also be stigmatizing and contribute to discrimination.

If we make guesses as to who may be suffering from what diagnosis, it can be damaging for those people. Moreover, our assumptions will also neglect the people who don't fit our stereotypes of being in need. In this book you have learned universal design approaches to accessibility. Therefore, you have resources to provide support to everyone without guessing who may need help and without anyone ever having to disclose their private mental health conditions to get what they need. That is important because many people would want that help but choose not to ask because they do not want others to know they have a mental health problem. It's also important because many people who will never qualify for a mental health diagnosis could still use support during conflicts.

Providing everyone with that support is simple. It means accepting that our role in these conflicts is to empower all of the people involved so that they can make their own decisions.

While it is not ideal for us to form ideas about whether someone has a mental illness and what might be best for them, it is inevitable that we will do so. Why? Because we are human beings. Our brains tell us stories about everyone we meet, and we automatically start making guesses and forming our own biased solutions. We need a clear process for compartmentalizing those thoughts and locking them somewhere else in our minds so that they do not ruin the conflict conversations we are having now.

You now have the tools that will help you create your process:

- You have recognized the complexity of mental health and have learned that people are entitled to make their own life decisions about it.

- You have learned empowering ways to talk about mental health in the relatively rare instance that someone chooses to start that conversation with you. You can use person-first language, open-ended questions, and reflective listening while you follow the other person's lead.

- You have been given roadmaps for being accessible and addressing challenging behaviors without singling anyone out and without linking these issues to mental illness stereotypes.

The skills of mental health communication, accessibility, and impartial challenging behavior planning are fundamental to combatting stigma and supporting empowerment. If you can commit to these three practices, you will be ready to help anyone get through their bad days without ever having to know whether they need that help at all.

By practicing these skills, you will be a better conflict practitioner during your own bad days too. Whenever your composure fails, your process will carry you through.

Takeaways

This section collects all of the takeaways from the book for your easy reference.

Part I: Understanding Mental Health Needs

Chapter 1: What Is Mental Health and Mental Illness?

- All needs can be seen as mental health needs, and everyone might have their own unique definition of mental health. Generally, mental health relates to all dimensions of well-being, with an emphasis on thoughts, feelings, and behaviors.

- Stay open to different ways that people may conceptualize their mental health problems, if they even see them as problems at all. Defer to their views and be sure to validate them.

- Mental health problems can be confusing and complicated. The DSM-5 is an imperfect labeling system used differently by different people. Avoid assumptions when you hear someone share their diagnosis, and instead listen to their choices and preferences.

- Regardless of whether you are worried about a person and whether you are worried about your legal liability, it is always important to show respect for someone's personal choices about their mental health.

- People have lots of decisions they can make about understanding, labeling, and treating mental health problems as well as choices about communication, support, and their overall lifestyle. Our role as conflict resolvers is to respect that these are their choices to make rather than assess if they are healthy. People can choose to get advice about what may help them from treatment professionals, assuming they choose to pursue that treatment. However, it is not our place to form judgments or give advice as part of a conflict resolution process. Nor is it our place to let our judgments of their decisions bias how we treat them.

- Remember that mental health is a world filled with options and choices, as opposed to definitive answers. If you offer options, respect that a person may not take advantage of them on your timeline if they ever do at all.

- People have unique, complex backgrounds, including their roles, cultures, and experiences surrounding mental health. These nuances help explain why many people have different mental health experiences and why it is important we validate any experiences anyone shares rather than assuming there are any "right" answers for them.

- Everyone you encounter has their own experiences that inform who they are and what choices they make. Some may have experienced trauma. These experiences are theirs to decide to share or keep private. We must always maintain an awareness that anyone could be impacted by any kind of positive or negative experience, that this may inform their behaviors, and that their experiences and choices are valid for them.

- A lot of different mental health terminologies mean different things to different people. Ask people what they mean rather than make assumptions.

- Fighting to convince someone to change their *beliefs* can be stigmatizing and counterproductive, while framing a conversation around their *choices* may lead everyone toward more fruitful, empowering discussions and agreements.

- Learning about mental disorders and mental health experiences can be dangerous if it leads you to form new biases and to act on these assumptions. You can never know what someone else is experiencing. Instead, focus on each person's choices and listen to what they share about their perspective and their history. Offer support universally without profiling based on mental health and respond to observed behaviors rather than guessing connections to mental health.

Chapter 2: How Do Mental Health Concerns Come Up in Disputes?

- If mental health information is already known but you were not given it directly, it is important that you do not factor that into your decision-making about offering process adjustments or addressing challenging behaviors. Also, do not ask about the condition just because you have learned about it. Lastly, do not assume your information is correct.

- Even when you believe you are aware of a mental health situation, your interpretations are not the full story. Keep an open mind rather than making assumptions.

- Focus on the behaviors that are related to your role in the situation, instead of bringing up the person's mental health situation. That behavior conversation could expand to include that person's mental health needs if they bring them up, but it doesn't have to. We should never aim to have that mental health conversation: it is the other person's decision whether they would like to have it or not.

- People disclose their mental health conditions for all sorts of reasons. Stay mindful that sharing a mental health problem does not in itself amount to a request for help and that assuming it does can lead to inadvertent paternalism and discrimination.

- At work, any request for a change, coupled with a potential medical need, may be a request for a reasonable accommodation.

- Accusations are very challenging. One approach is to use them as a reminder to share broad mental health practices and to model a shift away from mental health accusations toward the underlying behaviors that led to them.

- It is natural to have biases and to form guesses about someone's mental health, but it is vital to divorce those guesses from your decisions about how to manage conflicts. Follow a consistent process that does not single anyone out for different treatment based on suspected mental health problems, and you will reduce the chance that you inadvertently discriminate based on your decisions.

- Suspecting a mental health problem can lead you to act inappropriately. These suspicions can also stop you from addressing the real challenges you are facing. Avoid making these assumptions. Stay focused on your role, the process, and the behaviors you are observing.

- Suspicions can be about more than whether a diagnosis exists; they could also be about whether there is some instability now. Acting on these suspicions can lead to communication breakdowns, strained relationships, and estrangements. It is best to stay focused on peoples' choices and behaviors rather than get stuck in our assumptions.

Part II: Dispelling Myths about Mental Illness

Chapter 3: Why Are People Concerned?

- We're only human. Instead of beating ourselves up for our biases and mistakes, practice self-compassion and keep an open mind for opportunities for growth. We will never be perfectly impartial, but we can develop fairer processes in conflicts by following the principles in this book.

- Keep an open mind, challenge your assumptions, and avoid trusting your gut. Instead, follow universal, impartial processes for talking about mental health, addressing challenging behaviors, and being accessible to people's needs.

- To facilitate productive family conflict resolution, it may be best to focus on the behaviors and stop yourself from letting your assumptions guide you into a host of tangential, intractable conflicts.

- In workplace settings, focus on your role and on the behaviors that affect the workplace instead of assuming that mental health is involved with the challenging behaviors you are seeing.

- Unless your situation involves a commitment or guardianship dynamic, it is not appropriate to act paternalistically toward a person with a mental health problem. Even in those extreme situations where their choices are overridden, you can still use the techniques described in this book to treat them with respect and help them feel more empowered.

- Judging someone's beliefs or behavior as possibly related to a mental health problem and deciding to treat a person differently based on that perception is a form of paternalism that is inappropriate. Instead of acting paternalistically, focus on your actual role and on addressing challenging behaviors that fit your role.

- Unless clients have asked you to do a mental health assessment and offer tailored services, and it fits your role to do so, do not do one. Any changes you make based on that assessment are a source of bias.

- Stigma includes the negative attitudes inappropriately associated with a mental health condition. These attitudes can be extremely destructive, including the source of discrimination and negative internalized beliefs. Sadly, they are pervasive throughout our society.

- Although it can be difficult for someone with a mental health disability to complain due to stigma and the challenges demonstrating discrimination, labeling people can still provide evidence supporting a discrimination claim.

- Any policies that profile people based on an identity characteristic, such as the presence of mental health conditions, are stigmatizing. It is better to create policies based on behaviors.

- Sometimes people are not prepared for challenging behaviors or accessibility needs, and they end up believing that the problem is people who may have extra needs, such as people with mental illness. It is best to develop practices for responding to these challenging situations rather than scapegoating specific types of people.

- Scapegoating is dangerous. When people blame someone's mental health condition, it can become a big barrier to conflict resolution. It is best to stop scapegoating by expanding the conversation to broader framing of problems and remaining open-minded to many possibilities for understanding and resolving the issue.

Chapter 4: Do We Need to Label People?

- Whether labels end up being helpful or hurtful to people, it is not our role to be part of that process. Our role is to focus on the decisions people make regarding labels and follow their lead.

- Labels are imperfect, and they can disorient us or confuse a situation. Keep an open mind, listen, and trust people's choices instead of relying on labels.

- Labeling compromises impartiality and self-determination.

Chapter 5: Do People with Mental Health Problems Need Special Help?

- While it is good to be aware that anyone you are engaging with during a conflict may need help and while it is okay to generally offer resources for everyone, it is wrong to assume that someone specific needs help—especially in relation to their having a mental health condition.

- Deciding help for another person strips them of their autonomy. Keep them in the driver's seat; share options with them and let them choose and offer those options consistently to everyone.

- Even the most rigorous capacity assessments are flawed and are used in a biased manner, with people often questioning the capacity of people who disagree with them. Be very careful when assuming anyone lacks the capacity to make their own decisions.

- Everyone can benefit from help, and it is easiest for them to get it if we make broad, general offers of support to everyone in a conflict instead of trying to guess who might need assistance.

Chapter 6: Do People with Mental Health Problems Exhibit Challenging Behaviors?

- Associating dangerousness with mental health problems is fraught with error and inappropriate. Even if there were such an association, there is no unbiased or accurate way to predict this harm. Consequently, clinicians and others end up using their biased judgment to make these determinations.

- Screening out someone from a conflict resolution process is inappropriate if it is based on them having a mental health diagnosis. Instead, any process adjustments should be based solely on objective behavior criteria.

- Workplaces are breeding grounds for all sorts of toxic and nonproductive assumptions when mental health situations arise. Instead of succumbing to these imagined backstories or profiles about a person's disclosed mental health situation, focus on developing impartial responses to observable behaviors befitting everyone's role at work.

Part III: Best Practices for Empowerment

Chapter 7: Talk about Mental Health in an Empowering Way

- Whatever your role is, it is best to approach mental health conversations by deferring to each person's individual choices, focusing your contributions on validating their perspective and sharing objective behavior observations that are appropriate for you to comment on based on your specific role. These practices will help you empower people when you are discussing mental health.

- Use person-first language instead of defining a person by their mental health condition.

- Only ask about a person's mental health situation if they bring up the topic and limit your questions to what they decide to share. In these contexts, the best thing to do is to ask open-ended questions designed to let the person's choices dictate how you talk about mental health.

- Validating someone's perspective helps them feel heard and empowered. It does not require that you agree with their point of view, but only that you respect it.

- After you listen, it is helpful to say something to let the person know that you value their voice regardless of whether you disagree with their beliefs.

- Pay attention to the different choices involved in the conflict and emphasize them.

- Avoid sharing challenging information without permission and be sure to take the time to have the conversation in a way that feels empowering to the person you are engaging.

- Conflicts involving mental health needs involve positions and needs just like any other conflicts. Ask open ended questions to shift from positions and surface underlying needs. This will set the stage for brainstorming possible agreements.

- Reality-test agreements in conflicts involving mental health needs as you would any other agreements.

- Be ready to treat this conversation like any other, while also keeping in mind the lessons you learned to be sensitive to trauma, labels, sensitivities, and lifestyle choices.

- There are a lot of different ways families may choose to discuss mental health. Remember to emphasize and discuss their choices rather than assuming you know what they want.

Chapter 8: Develop Universal, Accessible Practices

- There are simple ways to offer help to everyone without singling out people with mental health conditions or other disabilities.

- The seven principles of universal design are a helpful tool for thinking of ways to design your conflict resolution process to meet everyone's mental health needs, rather than waiting for someone to ask for help. That is especially important so that people with mental health needs do not have to disclose them and thereby can avoid experiencing feelings of stigma.

- It can be relatively straightforward to incorporate universal design principles into your conflict resolution practices.

- Do not single people out with referrals to your health and wellness services. If you want to share resources, make general promotion efforts using consistent, universal criteria.

Chapter 9: Plan for Challenging Behaviors

- Challenging behaviors are common. When surveyed, conflict resolvers have indicated they want better plans for addressing them.

- Planning for challenging behaviors allows us to feel comfortable, be transparent, maximize safety, be fair, and correct our own fallibility.

- It is stigmatizing and nonproductive to use offensive labels such as "difficult people" instead of addressing challenging behaviors.

- Challenging behaviors can be categorized as emergencies, disruptions, and disconnects.

- Select which specific behavior is a problem and then describe it in objective terms without adding in your idea of any backstory.

- Plan ahead for challenging behaviors by identifying your prompt for action as well as the intervention you will use. The key is to use this plan instead of relying on your gut feelings.

Bonus Resources (2026 DRI Press Edition)

In honor of the 2025 DRI Press Edition of *Mental Health and Conflicts: A Handbook for Empowerment*, Dan Berstein and DRI Press have included the following additional resources:

The Mental Health Safe Project's Resource Collection for Mental Health and Conflicts

MH Safe has done a lot of work inspired by the lessons of this book, leading to many changes in the world of dispute resolution and beyond. Visit www.mhsafe.org/mhc to access:

- **Stigma and Conflict Resolution Resource Group Tools**
  These resources were created with funding from the NYC Department of Health and Mental Hygiene and the NY Office of Mental Health to help people use conflict resolution skills to prevent and address mental illness stigma, with a particular focus on helping them seek support, overcome rejection, and prevent mental illness discrimination
- **Trauma-Informed Response Initiative (TRI - pronounced "try") Resources**
  Inspired by Dan's experiences with the American Bar Association, MH Safe launched TRI to help people respond to challenging behaviors without writing anyone off. Access replays for Association for Conflict Resolution (ACR) programs on setting boundaries and addressing "bullying;" the Demystifying Distress event co-sponsored by Mediate.com, ACR, APFM, NAFCM, and CPR; and other related projects and tools.
- **Self-Advocacy Resources**
  See a list of changes and tools from MH Safe, and find areas where you can see how to respond to everyday mental illness discrimination; access addendum content to address inappropriate inquiries, impediments, and inaccessibilities; and report inappropriate publications.
- **Reader Surveys**
  Dan is writing a sequel book, *Mental Health and Conflicts: A Toolkit for Distress*, and a separate book *Bipolar Terror! Facing Fears and Freakouts About My Mental Illness*, each with surveys for readers to contribute their questions and examples.

Laboratory for Advancing Dispute Resolution Skills Teaching (DRI Skills Lab) Resources

DRI Skills Lab includes a searchable database of skills-based dispute resolution resources. Dan has contributed to the skills lab with exercises including the "Mental Illness Screening and Court Communication Role Play." Access the lab at https://mitchellhamline.edu/dri-skills-lab/ and that exercise at https://mitchellhamline.edu/dri-skills lab/mental-illness-screening-and-court-communication-role-play/

20 Years Embracing Bipolar

To celebrate his twenty year "bipolar-versary," marking the day he was first hospitalized and diagnosed with his mental illness, Dan compiled resources such as "Twenty Lessons from Twenty Years," a poem called "I Can Speak," and other items at a special new site: www.danberstein.com/20years

www.ingramcontent.com/pod-product-compliance
Lightning Source LLC
Chambersburg PA
CBHW081249040426
42452CB00015B/2764